A Victorian Guide
to Sex

To the brilliant Cyndsey,

Thank you so much

Up The Women!!

[signature]

For my family

A Victorian Guide to Sex

Fern Riddell

PEN & SWORD HISTORY

First published in Great Britain in 2014 by
PEN & SWORD HISTORY
an imprint of
Pen and Sword Books Ltd
47 Church Street
Barnsley
South Yorkshire S70 2AS

ISBN 978 1 78159 286 1

A CIP record for this book is available from the British Library.

Printed and bound in England by
CPI Group (UK) Ltd, Croydon, CR0 4YY

Typeset in Plantin by
CHIC GRAPHICS

Pen & Sword Books Ltd incorporates the imprints of
Pen & Sword Archaeology, Atlas, Aviation, Battleground, Discovery,
Family History, History, Maritime, Military, Naval, Politics, Railways,
Select, Social History, Transport, True Crime, and Claymore Press,
Frontline Books, Leo Cooper, Praetorian Press, Remember When,
Seaforth Publishing and Wharncliffe

For a complete list of Pen and Sword titles please contact
Pen and Sword Books Limited
47 Church Street, Barnsley, South Yorkshire, S70 2AS, England
E-mail: enquiries@pen-and-sword.co.uk
Website: www.pen-and-sword.co.uk

Contents

Acknowledgements

I would like to express my thanks to the staff at the British Library, to Rebecca Storr and Rory Cook of the Science Museum for their help and support in tracing all manner of surprising Victorian sexual ephemera, and to Dr Chris Naunton and the Egypt Exploration Society for the eleventh-hour Flinders Petrie revelations. I am grateful to both the British Newspaper Archive and Queen Victoria's Journals Online for allowing me to include quotations from their unique archives. Special thanks go to Beverley Cook of the Museum of London for her advice and knowledge, and my supervisor, Dr Paul Readman, for allowing me the precious time needed away from my PhD to complete this book.

To the community of historians around the world who have taken an interest in this book and who have continually sent me references and recipes – my grateful thanks. Charlie Tanner, Johanna Gummet and Fflur Huysmanns – your help and support were incredible. My gratitude also goes to John Gallagher and Maxime Ducrue for proofreading and translation. Any mistakes found in this book are my own.

I extend thanks to my brilliant editor, Jen Newby, to Steven Kirk for his beautiful illustrations, and to publishers Pen & Sword for being the first to take a chance on a new author.

I dedicate this book to my family.

The Society of Social Morality presents a selection of volumes
Taken from the accounts of its meetings
For the furthering of knowledge and
Human social understanding.

Introduction

The Victorians – Societies and Their Purpose –
W.T. Stead and Modern Babylon – The Contagious Diseases Acts –
Our Honest Narrators

Right from the start, let's get one thing perfectly clear. The Victorians really enjoyed sex. They wrote about it, they talked about it, they analysed it and they worried about it just as much as we do today. Until now, it seems as if most of our ideas about sex and the Victorians have been pretty one-dimensional. It's all prostitutes, porn and prudery, with very little left over for the everyday lives of your average Victorian.

But while the history books have fallen over themselves to ridicule a number of well-to-do ladies fainting at uncovered table legs, Queen Victoria, and a black-toothed erstwhile East End girl out for a good time, what was the actual reality of sex advice in the 1800s? It's very simple – the Victorians wanted to know how to have sex, when to have sex and – most importantly – how to enjoy sex, not normally something history has taught us to associate with our great-great-great-grandparents.

From describing the morally dangerous anatomical museums to revealing the ingenious use of a gentleman's top hat in the *Femme de Voyage*, this book brings together the huge diversity of advice you can find in the pamphlets, literature, newspapers and medical books of the nineteenth century and presents it as if it is a single volume from the period. Written in the style of the age, each chapter has its own unique narrator to guide you through the weird, the wonderful and the occasionally warped ideas the Victorians had about sex.

So why have the Victorians got such a bad reputation…?

Illustrated Police News, 18 September 1897. Image © THE BRITISH LIBRARY BOARD. ALL RIGHTS RESERVED. Image reproduced with kind permission of The British Newspaper Archive (www.british newspaperarchive.co.uk).

Introduction

So, whether you are interested in a doctor's view of the human body; the dating advice for single men and women; making your marriage a success; giving birth to beautiful children; or the practical elements, from contraception to STDs and sexual aids, everything that the Victorians wanted to know about sex is in the pages of this book.

So why have the Victorians got such a bad reputation when it comes to sex? Why do we only think of them as sexually repressed or sexually explicit? The answer, I think, has to come from human memory. We have a tendency to remember only the very best of times, or the very worst, and history (or the writing of history) tends to follow the same rules. So the most extreme events, people and attitudes are the ones that have been written about and repeated. No one really cares that Mr. and Mrs. Smith of No. 24 were having an enjoyable and healthy sex life if their neighbours were either living a life of debauchery and sin or pious chastity. And this is how historical misinformation happens – the extremes are repeatedly discussed and taken to be the attitudes of everyone who lived at that time. So what were people's sexual attitudes, ideas and practices for the *whole* Victorian era? This is what I want to explore – and the historical reality is really quite surprising.

The Victorians were dedicated to the idea of mutual physical sexual fulfilment, albeit within the boundaries of married life. Although sex outside marriage was seen in a negative light by the press and popular opinion, sex within marriage was hugely important. Finding the right person who would physically match you and with whom you could spend the rest of your life was driven by one single idea: True Love. That sounds pretty modern to me. The quest to find the right person with whom you can have a physically rewarding relationship and create a home and family is still argued about and discussed in great detail by our literature and society, although we tend to use blogs and TV shows whereas the

Library of Congress, early 1900s

Victorians used pamphlets and treatises.

Of all the surprisingly modern things the Victorians thought about sex, the one element that I never expected to find was their knowledge and understanding of the female orgasm. As far as the Victorians were concerned, especially at the beginning of the nineteenth century, the only way a woman could become pregnant was if she experienced an orgasm at the same time as her lover. So ideas of female sexual pleasure, and advice for getting it right, were written about and shared throughout the century, which really makes the Victorians just like us – just as worried about how to find that 'right' person, just as worried about married life and just as worried about how to have a happy and healthy sexual relationship.

Just like us, the Victorians were hugely preoccupied and worried by the sex industry – should it be legitimised? Should it be repressed? How do we protect the women within it? How do we stop the horrors of trafficking and child prostitution? Throughout the nineteenth century this issue is continually in the press, in parliament and in public, as prostitution and the trade of sex by both men and women was regularly exposed and exploited by different factions within society. There are huge moments of success, such as the campaign against the trade of young girls begun by W.T. Stead, culminating in the age of consent being raised from 13 to 16 in 1885, but there are also huge moments of horrific repression. This was exposed when Josephine Butler fought against the Contagious Diseases Acts of the 1860s, which allowed women to be forcibly examined and incarcerated in a locked ward if they were suspected of carrying any sexually transmitted diseases. The Victorian period is full of things we can understand and ideas, attitudes, and objects that seem utterly alien. But isn't that what exploring history is all about?

There is one inescapable Victorian attitude that modern day audiences might find difficult to understand and that is their total fear of the dangers involved with the practice of *onanism*, or, as we would say, masturbation. Previous cultures have had quite a laid-back approach to masturbation – the ancient Egyptians dedicated statues to the ithyphallic God Min, depicted with an erect penis – but in 1760 Samuel Tissot published *L'Onanisme* in which he set out the medical implications of indulging in what the Victorians would call 'The Solitary Vice' to be either insanity or death. Now, that might sound ridiculous to us, but to the Victorians it was a fear that dominated their medical textbooks, their marriage guides and their advice on morals and manners. But just because they were told *not* to do it, doesn't mean it didn't happen. Masturbation features in the erotica and pornography from the period and it was clearly as much a part of sexual interaction then, as it is now.

So, much of what we think we know about the Victorians and sex happens towards the end of the nineteenth century – Jack the Ripper reveals the horrors of Victorian prostitution; the trial of Oscar Wilde places a spotlight on gay culture in the metropolis; and Dr. Mortimer Grandville invents the first electric muscular massage, but what happened before that?

Introduction

Much of what we know about the Victorians comes from the work of the societies who campaigned for social reform. In the time before the welfare state, the protection of the people most at risk in society was dealt with by groups of like-minded individuals, normally from the upper and middle classes, who wanted to control and protect ideas of marriage, sex, and social interaction. One of the earliest of these was the puritanically named 'Society for the Suppression of Vice' – similar to my own 'Society of Social Morality' and the characters who will guide you through this book – which was established in 1802 with the help of William Wilberforce, one of the leading campaigners for the abolition of slavery. This society was driven by the belief that lewd talk, drunkenness, swearing, obscene books and prints, brothels and gaming houses should be outlawed in decent society. While that might sound as if they really just didn't want anyone to have any fun, societies such as this occupied an important role as the moral barometers of the Victorian world, telling them what was, and what wasn't considered acceptable. The society was active throughout the Victorian period and became part of the National Vigilance Association in 1885.

How the Victorians censored their world, and what they considered to be immoral, is hugely important when understanding their changing attitudes towards sex and why we see them as so sexually restrained. Due to the work of the Society for the Suppression of Vice – and other organisations such as the Society for the Rescue of Young Women and Children, which was set up in the 1850s – we have the laws in place today to protect those most at risk. Before governmental bodies were set up to examine and prosecute people involved in sex trafficking, it was the members of organisations like the Society for the Rescue of Young Women and Children who would send their members – both men and women – across the country, and even the world, to investigate the traffickers and bring them to justice. You can read more about the trafficking scandals in *Lord Arthur Cleveland's Extreme Tastes* – just don't hold me responsible for his view of them.

So public discussions on sex in the nineteenth century involve a constant balancing act between moral panic and moral reform – panic about uncontrolled sexual desires and reform to protect those who were not able to protect themselves.

But why did anyone care? Or why is it that the Victorians seemed to care more than those in previous centuries about legislating sexual morality and immorality? The nineteenth century had seen a huge explosion in industrialisation and urbanisation across the world. From the establishment of the United States to Isambard Kingdom Brunel's advances in engineering and

Charles Darwin's publication of his theories on evolution and the origin of species, the nineteenth century exploded with new ideas and new experiences unlike any that had gone before. The locomotive railways of the 1820s paved the way for the railways we know today and discoveries in the fields of science and archaeology fractured long-held and traditional beliefs about the way the world worked and a human being's role within it. A huge preoccupation of the nineteenth century was trying to understand where you now fitted into this new world and what being 'modern' really meant.

For the Victorians, part of this understanding came from controlled investigation. The Industrial Revolution had brought about large-scale population redistribution away from the rural communities of the previous centuries and into the towns and cities. This meant that many people lived in very close and confined quarters, which provided the perfect conditions for mass observation – exploring the tastes, attitudes and lives of as many people as possible. One of the earliest social investigators was Henry Mayhew (1812–1887) whose 1851 work, *London Labour and the London Poor,* laid the groundwork for all who would come after him, as he brought the hitherto hidden lives of London's working-class communities to the knowledge of the rest of Victorian society. Mayhew's richly coloured texts exposed in glorious detail the lives of the urban poor – from costermongers to game hawkers, flower girls to sham street sellers, pickpockets and prostitutes – as this description of the Brill Sunday morning market shows:

As you enter the Brill the market sounds are scarcely heard. But at each step the low hum grows gradually into the noisy shouting, until at last the different cries become distinct, and the hubbub, din, and confusion of a thousand voices bellowing at once again fill the air. The road and footpath are crowded, as on the over-night; the men are standing in groups, smoking and talking; whilst the women run to and fro, some with the white round turnips showing out of their filled aprons, others with cabbages under their arms, and a piece of red meat dangling from their hands. Only a few of the shops are closed, but the butcher's and the coal-shed are filled with customers, and from the door of the shut-up baker's, the women come streaming forth with bags of flour in their hands, while men sally from the halfpenny barber's smoothing their clean-shaved chins. Walnuts, blacking, apples, onions, braces, combs, turnips, herrings, pens, and corn-plaster, are all bellowed out at the same time. Labourers and mechanics, still unshorn and undressed, hang about with their hands in their pockets, some with their pet terriers under their arms. The pavement is green with the refuse leaves of vegetables, and round a cabbage-barrow the women stand turning over the bunches, as the man shouts, 'Where you like, only a penny.' Boys are running home with the breakfast herring held in a piece of paper, and the side-pocket of the apple-man's stuff coat hangs down with the weight of the halfpence stored within it.

Not even Dickens is so able to bring the sights and sounds of Victorian London to life with the same intensity as Mayhew, and for its readers, it brought a wealth of interest into the attitudes and experiences of people normally ignored by history – the poor. And what did the poor seem to do far more than everyone else? Have children. Which must mean they are having sex, which must mean sex needs to be controlled so that we have fewer poor children. Or at least that was what the *Victorians* thought.

Sex in the nineteenth century isn't just about human interaction, it is also about the wider fears of a population increase, sexual manipulation and what was happening on your doorstep. When Charles Booth published *Life and the Labour of the People in London* in 1889, he included a map of every street in

Illustrated Police News, 12 September 1885

London, colour-coded from the most criminal and poverty-stricken to the most wealthy. Suddenly, every Londoner was able to see the area they lived and worked in compared with that of their neighbours. But London had been a divided metropolis long before Booth published his map. The designated areas of the Haymarket and Whitechapel were known as the haunts of prostitutes and home to brothels. The impact of the social investigators was to take those places, previously gossiped about and avoided by the respectable members of society, and publically acknowledged their location. This rendered them unavoidable and if society can't ignore something then it has to be dealt with.

When W.T. Stead opened the pages of the *Pall Mall Gazette* on the morning of 6 July 1885, I wonder if he had accurately guessed the extent of the public outcry that was about to greet his first instalment of 'The Maiden Tribute of Modern Babylon'. Here, in lurid detail, Stead recounted his successful attempt at finding and procuring a young 13-year-old girl for sex. His readers were outraged. Stead exposed the horrors of child prostitution, from an alcoholic mother willing to sell her daughter for £5, to the drugging and removal of the child to a house of disrepute where she was left to await the mercies of her buyer. But why had he written it? Was it purely for sensationalism and to sell newspapers, or was there a more noble motivation?

Born in Northumberland in 1854, Stead became the editor of his first newspaper, *The Northern Echo,* at the tender age of 22 and quickly built a reputation as a newspaper man. He wrote in a style which Matthew Arnold, noted poet of the time, christened 'New Journalism' – which was not the compliment it might sound. Arnold had been a previous contributor before Stead took over the editorship of the *Pall Mall Gazette* in 1883 and disliked the muckraking which Stead – and his readers – found so interesting. New Journalism, which was similar to the tabloid journalism of today, was seen as nothing more 'than literary "eye-openers", more or less vulgar, more or less lying'. But it was the investigation into child prostitution that would secure Stead's position in the history books, and 'The Maiden Tribute to Modern Babylon' would echo across the centuries and into the modern world.

Some say it was the influence of Charles Booth that directed Stead towards an exposé of child prostitution in the capital, but it was with the help of another Booth, Bramwell Booth, that Stead launched his investigation. Bramwell was the son of The Salvation Army founder, William Booth, and occupied the role of Chief of Staff in the organisation. It was to Bramwell that Stead turned to investigate the Victorian underbelly and find the connections that would lead to those involved in the trafficking of young girls.

Since the formation of The Salvation Army in 1865, Salvation Army members working in the East End regularly attempted to rescue young women and girls who had fallen into prostitution, and Booth and Stead manipulated those relationships until they found a woman who would provide them with the information they required. Rebecca Jarrett, a reformed brothel-keeper, agreed to aid them in their search and, after a while, located the Armstrong family and their 13-year-old daughter, Eliza. What happened next remains a mystery, but at some point, whether (as Eliza's mother claimed) Rebecca offered Eliza a job in service, or (as Rebecca claimed) Eliza's mother agreed to sell her daughter into prostitution, the sum of £5 changed hands and Eliza was then drugged and removed from her family.

Stead then claimed she was taken to a place to await his visitation so that the procedure of buying a young girl and removing her to a place of immoral actions could have been simulated. In 'Modern Babylon' Stead claimed he waited in the room with Eliza until she woke up and, on seeing him, she screamed. He then left the room and Eliza was taken by Rebecca to a respectable situation in Paris where she was cared for until the consequences of Stead's articles became clear.

These took two forms: The Criminal Law Amendment Act of 1885, which had shown signs of wavering, was pushed through less than a month later by the public outrage that greeted Stead's exposé. Created for the 'protection of

Illustrated Police News, 21 November, 1885.

women and children', the bill raised the age of consent from 13 to 16 and enforced harsh penalties against anyone involved in the procurement or transportation of young women for sex. It was a huge victory. But there was another, possibly unforeseen, consequence of the passing of the bill. It made all of Stead's actions a criminal offence.

Stead, Booth, Rebecca and three others were charged with the abduction of Eliza, the unlawful administering of a noxious drug and indecent assault. Although Stead had disguised her name in his articles, by September 1885 – a month after the Act had been passed and two months after his original publications – Eliza Armstrong's name was everywhere. The court was besieged by applicants wanting to witness the trial – from Eliza's mother tearfully stating that she had not been informed of her daughter's removal for immoral purposes and insisting that she had visited Mr Booth to be assured of Eliza's welfare (Booth having offered to show her a certificate that Eliza had left for Paris a virgin, and had certainly not been molested in any way) – to Eliza's very own testimony. She had enjoyed her life in Paris, and at no time had suspected that she had been removed from her family for any other reason than employment, although, on leaving her in Paris, Rebecca Jarrett had told her that her mother had agreed to let her go, and for immoral purposes, but Eliza had refused to believe her. There is something sadly innocent about Eliza's evidence. Although her case brought attention to very real and horrifying issues in the Victorian period, she does seem to have been unwittingly manipulated by adult figures desperately using her to prove their own arguments.

After the trial it was only Booth who escaped without sentence: Stead received three months; Rebecca, six. But it did little to quell Stead's 'New Journalism' investigations and he continued to write and publish on social sexual control until his death on board the *Titanic* in 1912. But Stead was not alone in his desire to further the protection of women and children in the nineteenth century and the actions of one woman influenced him more than any other.

Josephine Butler is a name few know, but all should cherish. Her attack on the Contagious Diseases Acts of the 1860s highlights one of the worst forms of sexual legislation that has ever been passed in Britain. First brought into law in 1864, and then again in 1866 and 1869, the Contagious Diseases Act was an attempt by the government to regulate and control the spread of venereal disease through its population. A report into the diseases suffered by the armed forces had highlighted that a large percentage of the men suffered from a sexually transmitted disease, often either syphilis or gonorrhoea. In 1860 the rate of infection was so bad that *The Lancet* declared that of those stationed in

Portsmouth, '508 of every 1000 men, one in every two, were venereal patients'.

Clearly, something had to be done, and for the government the answer lay in the passing of the Contagious Diseases Acts. But, instead of legislating the men, punishing them for immoral sexual interactions and visiting prostitutes, or providing education and medical aid to those suffering, the Contagious Diseases Acts targeted women. This was because of an old-fashioned idea common in the early Victorian period – and frighteningly echoed by some discussions surrounding the sex industry today – that prostitutes were required by men to protect virtuous women from men's uncontrollable lusts. Men were not able to control themselves and needed access to public women – prostitutes – for the safety of society. So it was women who were seen as the carriers of the disease, not men, and it was the women who had to be controlled.

The Contagious Diseases Acts allowed for any woman to be forcibly examined for symptoms of venereal disease if a policeman suspected that she might be carrying the disease. Often, this was targeted at known prostitutes, but all that was needed for the examination to be carried out was the officer's belief that the woman 'might' be infected, whether or not she was known locally as a prostitute. Little or no evidence was provided other than the policeman's word. The woman was then ordered to appear before a magistrate, who would decide whether or not the examination should take place and, if he decided to allow it, he would order her to be examined by a doctor. If she was found to have any symptoms of venereal disease, or the doctor suspected she might show them later, the woman was immediately removed to a lock hospital or locked ward. Here she would remain for three to nine months, with little or no contact with the world outside. Lock hospitals were exactly as their name suggests, wards specifically for the treatment of sexual diseases, from which there was no escape.

When the Acts were first enforced they were passed with little opposition, applying only to port and barracks towns, and heavily couched in the language of social improvement. It was for the benefit of the health of the population, protection against the social evil of prostitution. Given that many of the women targeted were working class, little interest was taken in their welfare. But by 1869, when the boundaries of the Acts were extended to the civil population and stories of horrifying episodes – in which women seemed just to disappear from the streets – began to be published in the press, the terrifying realities of life under the Contagious Diseases Acts became apparent.

There was an immediate response: The Ladies National Association for The Repeal of the Contagious Diseases Acts was founded, launching a frank and honest discussion on the relationship between men and women and the sex industry at its meetings, in pamphlets, and the national press. 'An Englishwoman' wrote of the need and motivations of the Ladies National Association (LNA) in the *London Daily News* published in 1869:

> *Permit me to explain, in a brief but careful way, what the danger is in which we find our country and everybody in it involved, through the ignorance and carelessness of whole classes of our countrymen, whose duty it is to know better, the apathy of legislators who have permitted the destruction of our most distinctive liberties before their eyes, and the gross prejudices and coarse habits of thought of professional men who have been treated as oracles on a subject on which they are proved mistaken at every turn.*

The tone of her writing expresses the violent anger many women felt at the loss of liberties and the double standards that they were subjected to under the Acts. This was not an attack on a class or profession of women, this was an attack on womankind. The LNA began a long and loud campaign to expose the truth of the Acts, from their basis in poor statistics to the punishment of women in what was – to the Victorians – a very male sin, that of physical sexual lust. For 20 years, one of the Ladies National Association founding members, Josephine Butler, was at the forefront of the campaign for the repeal of the Acts. She was one of the earliest female social investigators, heading into the towns and ports where the Acts were enforced in order to bring back the stories of the women who suffered under them. They were published in *The Shield*, as well as in the national press, and exposed not only the women's experiences, but also those of the common soldiers and naval men.

Working-class men and women who did not seek a legal marriage, but who often lived in committed lifelong common-law marriages, were also targeted by the enforcers of the Acts. Although they lived what society would have regarded as 'respectable' lives, the lack of a legal marriage meant that they were punished and degraded under the Acts, whereby enforcers could seize the women and remove them for months at a time. The risk of this happening to a woman who was not a prostitute was increased with the creation of a task force of special constables, sent down from London to oversee and enforce the Acts on the local populace.

Josephine took her campaign to international levels, travelling across Europe to build international pressure on a British government who refused to admit the Acts were the most 'conspicuous disgrace of our time'. After many years of vilification, in 1886 the repeal campaign was finally successful, owing much, if not all, to her tenacity and dedication. She was an exceptional woman, uniting women in the fight for their own freedoms and liberties long before the Suffragette Movement even began. You can learn more about her from Mrs. Dollymop in 'Advice for Single Ladies'.

It's against the backdrop of these two moments of sexual reform and legislation – headed by Stead and Butler – that the Victorians explored and examined their attitudes to sex. From the marriage guides and pamphlets that were published continually throughout the nineteenth century, to the hotly debated medical ideas, and reports in the newspapers, sex was rarely out of the public gaze. Every single piece of advice contained within this book has been collected from the wealth of those sources. Instead of presenting *A Victorian Guide to Sex* chronologically, I've set it out thematically, to give you a real flavour of what was available to the Victorians throughout their century.

We collect information throughout our lifetimes, never knowing when it may become relevant to us. Sex advice can be passed down from generation to generation, or friend to friend, and this gives it an almost timeless quality, as you can never really be sure how old, or how new, the ideas you encounter might be. We know the Victorians were great collectors and classifiers – most of our museums house collections they created – and that attitude can be seen in their approach to sex. Ideas from earlier centuries are stacked up next to the modern medical discoveries, and everything, *everything*, is investigated.

What may surprise you about the Victorians is not how different to us they are, but actually how *similar* their ideas might be. And so this leads me to the book you are now reading. Let's begin with a quick description of your narrators, who will guide you from here on in. I have brought them together as if they are the members of the fictitious Society of Social Morality, to offer the advice to their members on all things sexual. Published annals of a society's activities were not uncommon, and while this society and its characters are my own invention, everything they describe, each object, attitude and idea, is authentically Victorian.

The first person you will meet is Dr. Dimmick and for me, he is representative of that great Victorian showman, the quack doctor. He may, at some point, have been a showman, or a strongman, as his dedication to health and the physical figure might suggest. But in recent memory he has given himself to providing a clear and accurate guide to the physical anatomy of the human body and how that will influence your choice of a mate. With an understanding of sexual desire; the purpose of menstruation; and the many risks and dangers to your health from the practice of celibacy and masturbation, the good doctor will set out all the medical knowledge he has at his disposal.

However, given he was a devotee of that spectacular moment of Victorian bad science known as physiognomy, I'm not sure how far to trust his 'medical' credentials. Indeed, as legitimate qualifications for medical men became standardised during the Victorian period, the number of quack doctors – or fake doctors – began to go into decline. They had often specialised in patent medicines, or general-purpose ointments and pills, which claimed to cure everything from colds to cancer. One such man was Thomas Holloway, who began creating his general-purpose ointment in 1837 and who manufactured it until his death in 1883. He managed to accrue a huge fortune from the sale of his products and was responsible for the stunning building of Royal Holloway College in 1879, which was officially opened to its female students in 1886. I like to think he would have inspired Dimmick.

Mrs. Dollymop has clearly never legally been married. After an active youth in bohemian Paris, her adult life has been spent in service to the young ladies of her school, where she has watched many come and go. But she has never lost faith in the institution of marriage, or in love. Her advice ranges from ideas of womanhood, fashion choices, health, the importance of a padded bust and flirtation to that most central of virtues of the Victorian woman: the importance of being yourself. She briefly discusses when to marry and the considerations of choosing the right husband, but ends with some important lessons to be learnt from the lives of Victorian women.

Women have often been painted into a very submissive role where sex in the nineteenth century is concerned, either depicted as desperately trying to live up to an impossible male-imagined ideal of the perfect wife and mother, or as fallen women, again the result of male attitudes towards women and prostitution. Neither of these ideals reflect women in any light other than as victims. But the Victorian period was full of incredible women, women like Josephine Butler, who fought hard for their place on an equal footing with men. The campaign for women's right to vote began in the nineteenth century and it was women's determination to protect their own sex from discrimination and sexual predation that drove much of the campaigns for social reform. Women did *not* have a passive role where sex was concerned.

The Reverend J.J. James is one of my favourite characters, although he doesn't have much to say, rather, I think, suffering under the impression that young men don't really listen to you anyway. Religion is something I have avoided tackling, believing that it has little to do with the act of sex outside of its perceived legitimisation. For the Victorians, religion, and the place of religion, was in dramatic flux after Darwin and it was also surprisingly absent from much of the material I examined. But whilst it may not have had a practical application to sex, it was the driving force behind many of the social reformers, who sought to rescue nineteenth-century society from its vice-ridden existence and to create a new moral utopia.

The Reverend offers his young charges advice on manliness, holding up the physical perfection of Eugen Sandow – known as the 'Monarch of Muscle' – as someone to aspire to. He dispenses wisdom on courtship and flirtations and the ever faithful practical guide on how to choose your wife by the shape of her legs, as well as notes on the wedding day itself. For those less willing to abide by society's rules and who indulge in fornication before a marriage has taken place, he can offer some methods of contraception – protection also – against any connections that might result in a nasty infection.

Lady Petronella Von-Hathsburg was, at one time, a great society beauty, but she has gone to seed a little in the resulting years, after a very happy marriage to her much beloved, and lately departed husband. Her enjoyment of the good life is something she advises in moderation, but then I have never felt she believes very heavily in practising what one preaches. Her thoughts on marriage, after many successful decades as both wife and mother, are unsurpassed. She outlines the roles of husband and wife, tackles the question of a woman's inferiority, and gives advice on establishing – and then somehow maintaining – matrimonial harmony. But of greater importance are her practical efforts to discuss sex itself.

From Victorian foreplay to the art of conception, her knowledge encompasses methods to combat sterility, pleasure and pregnancy, as well as when it is least advisable to have sex. Finally, she sets out what is needed for a lasting happy family life, and, should all else fail, considers the subject of divorce. This may be the most surprising of volumes, as it deals very much with the realities of sex in the Victorian period without the taint of criminality or social disapproval. This is how to have sex and how to enjoy sex as the Victorians would have wanted.

Mr. Mandrake, the continually nervous chemist, walks a fine tightrope between what is legal and what is illegal. Although he may offer you medical aid for all your sexual woes, I have never been able to shake off the nagging feeling that, should you appear to be of a discreet nature, his back room, accessed from behind the counter and through a faded red velvet curtain, will hold a number of objects surely at risk of being confiscated by the police. Pills and solutions he has aplenty and cures for gonorrhoea, syphilis, gleet and hysteria. He will espouse his knowledge of massage and the best practice of it, as well as the devices available to aid you with its effects – all of which come fitted for the new art of 'vibration'.

And when the light is low, or perhaps the shop is empty, he will direct you to a perusal of his latest 'Parisian Rubber Articles'. From the *Femme de Voyage* to the *Ladies Syringe*, he also stocks a number of other practical aids: an ivory carved phallus (with plunger), Baundruches – with the faces of notable personages painted on the front – and preventative rings with their sharply pointed metal teeth, perfect for a gentleman with untameable urges.

Lord Arthur Cleveland has not been, nor will he ever be, a good man. He has indulged in every vice and fetish it has been possible for him to find, is a regular of the East End girls, and possibly the West End boys, and his memoirs demonstrate the darker side of sexual life in the Victorian period. From brothels such as Madam D'Alma's, the trafficking of Chinese girls in railway crates, and prostitutes and their practices, to the early sexual experiences of a young man, Lord Arthur will lead you through some of the worst sexual attitudes of the nineteenth century. The attitudes of the rich and the belief that the upper classes preyed sexually on the weaker members of society – from working-class prostitutes to respectable serving girls – were rife throughout the time that Victoria was on the throne.

As the nineteenth century drew to a close, the attacks of Jack the Ripper and the revelations during Oscar Wilde's trial for sodomy focused those fears on class victimisation. And when we find out, after Princess Alexandra purchases 'Vigor's Horse-Action Saddle', that her husband and heir to the throne, Prince Albert Edward, had a sexual predilection for custom-built furniture, the sexual practices of the rich seem to swing very much into focus.

Victorian societies were at the heart of much of the social reform in this period, and each member of the fictitious Society of Social Morality exposes the humorous and confusing ideas the nineteenth century had throughout its history. The volumes compiled here are the Annals of the Society and within them, every facet of Victorian sexuality can be explored. Discover, perhaps for the first time, the wealth of knowledge, the bizarre ideas and the unique practices of the Victorians, and see for yourself just how like them we really are...

Dr Dimmick's Anatomy of the Human Body

Anatomical Museums – The Role of the Sexual Organs –
A Few Words on Puberty – Menstruation – Sexual Love in the Young –
Sexual Desire – The Invariable Risks of Celibacy – The Marriage Age –
The Practice of Physiognomy – Masculine Women and
Effeminate Men – Masturbation – Disease

SIRS! Ladies! Allow me to impart the years of knowledge my medical calling has bestowed upon me. Within these pages I will reveal the mysteries of the human body; the secrets contained within those organs most revered for their life-creating properties; the dangers of untamed sexual desire; and the urgings that are present in all men, and all *women*. I will reveal to you, O captive Reader, the changes experienced by all who seek to fulfil their natural desires and the bodily and emotional differences felt by either sex. Take comfort in this, the most up-to-date and modern of volumes, which will satisfy any question you may wish to be answered, with the best and wisest of medical experience.

Any discussion on the anatomy of the human body can only begin with the physical differences of the flesh. For those who wish to delve deeper into the physical differences between each sex, I would willingly advise you to wander your way to that most celebrated of collections currently housed at 315 Oxford Street. Therein, you will discover the *Anatomical Theatre of the illustrious German doctor, Joseph Kahn. Formerly 'Dr. Kahn's Anatomical Museum'*, which once occupied three apartments at the Portland Rooms, and previously '*Dr. Kahn's New Museum and Gallery of Science*', in Tichborne Street.

The exhibit has now been housed permanently on Oxford Street, clearly accessible for all who wish to visit it. Inside there is the most informed and diverse exhibition of physiology, anatomy and pathology, exploring a wide variety of medical subjects; the development of the human form from its earliest stage; the growth of the bones; the five senses that are most astoundingly dissected; diseases resulting from sexual connection; specimens of human and animal brain, allowing for the most intriguing moments of comparative anatomy; and numerous heads, moulded and coloured, to demonstrate the sanguineous, phlegmatic and bilious temperaments. When they were first exhibited, a number of microscopic specimens from the world of embryology drew much comment from medical men, and I would allow that this demonstrates that each object has been placed in the collection by virtue of its purely educational and scientific nature. There is nothing to offend your sensibilities, only to arouse your curiosities.

For any student of physiology, a visit to this – the most popular of Anatomical Museums – is beyond compare. Indeed, *The Lancet*, which we know to be the leading medical journal of our time, gave the most empathic of recent declarations, '*Altogether it is a splendid scientific collection, and a great deal of general information is to be obtained by a visit.*' Such a collection is unique in construction, and – I would say – most masterly mapped out. Although some have seen fit to malign it with condemnations in the press, you have my word that there is not a hint of vulgarity or sensuality in any part of the collection.

Does not Guy's Hospital have its own Museum of a similar purpose? It houses over 10,000 specimens, 4,000 drawings and diagrams, as well as a supposedly unique collection of Anatomical Models, and a series of 500 models of skin diseases. That establishment is for the benefit of those who wish to become a student at Guy's, whose medical education – after submittal of a satisfactory statement of their education and conduct – will be covered by a fee of £40 for the first year, £40 for the second, and £10 for every succeeding year of attendance; or £100 in one payment which will entitle the student to a perpetual ticket.

But what of my readers who have yet to venture towards our noble capital? Fear not, for Anatomical Museums can be found across our fair nation! I happened to chance across the '*Berlin Collection of Anatomy*' on an 1874 excursion to Manchester. As I clutched the playbill proffered to me outside the new Town Hall, I was suspicious of the advertised '*beautiful figures, brought from Paris, Florence, and Munich*', not believing them to be in any way comparable with those we see so readily in London.

But I was most surprised to find that the figures were indeed more than worthy to be judged against those held in my own, dearest, city. I would be as bold as to say I was awe-struck by the delicate specimens, which laid bare every vital organ of the human body in wax and other forms. Cards placed beside the specimens bore such mottos as '*Educate the mind and the body will be educated*'; '*Knowledge is Power*'; and most important of all, '*to the pure all things are pure*'. Thursdays were specifically set aside for ladies, and when regarding all of this I could see no flaw nor find any fault or malice in the exhibition's design. I was most disappointed to learn the museum was raided some time later and its collection seized by the police on unfounded grounds of immorality.

There has been a subtle change in recent years by those within the medical profession and in league with the Society for the Suppression of Vice, to brand our beloved public museums of anatomy as '*filthy, obscene, and indecent*' and '*calculated to offend public decency and demoralise society*'. Two surgeons, a Mr. Wright and a Mr. Law, reportedly used words to this effect before a grand jury on the subject. I cannot help but wonder what benefit this has been towards the medical profession, to remove from all persons the most gentle and innocent knowledge of their own human body. I heard recently of a prosecution brought against Mr. Joseph Woodhead, proprietor of an anatomical museum in Sheffield, whose figures were now deemed to be dangerous and immoral in their display.

I was greatly surprised to hear of this, as Mr. Woodhead's figures were first exhibited at the Great Exhibition in London in 1851. Indeed, it was there that the most respectable members of society, including those of royalty, had viewed the models and the figures elicited great praise from the newspapers. There seems to be a most strange and unwelcome change in the mood of our society, one that seeks to restrict every man and woman, from every class, from an understanding of the very form we all inhabit. Unless you have the ability to secure an education in the medical profession, I fear you will soon be denied the knowledge previous generations obtained with ease!

So what of those who seek answers, unfettered by complicated and confusing medical language? What of those who fear the medical man and his secrets? This volume, which I thank the generous members of the society for allowing me to write, will set out all those questions the human mind asks as it grows from child to adult. I will focus on those physical aspects most relevant to the sexual organs and their activities; the journey through puberty; the irregularities faced by women; physiognomy and its importance to marriage; sexual immorality; and the disease risked by all who engage in illicit activities. My own life has allowed me to be most engaged with such study and my years as a medical man qualify the judgements that I will impart to you to be of the most learned and studious in character.

The Role of the Sexual Organs: -

The human species consists of two main elements, that of masculine and that of feminine. The masculine element we well know to be represented by wisdom, a certain majesty, and force, whilst the feminine element has always represented itself in grace, beauty, devotion, love, patience and intuition. It is the physical combination of these two elements, that of male and female, that allows us to indulge in the *act of generation* and so create a family line. This is only achieved with the proper understanding of sexual passion, that most natural and human of urges. All love between the sexes is based upon this sexual passion, but its manifestations, which can be numerous and utterly incomparable, will always be solely determined by the coarseness or refinement of the individuals concerned. Those persons who are of a coarse animal nature can exhibit only a coarse animal love.

There are those who believe that the reproductive organs have a single and sole use, that of the propagation of the species. But, whilst it is true that every part of the human economy has its own particular use, the sexual organs encompass several:

1. They are the most willing assistant in the resolving of animal passions.
2. They afford an outlet of accumulated secretion.
3. They are the secret incentive to sexual love.
4. They are the bond of union between the sexes.

There is an appetite created within them, similar to the state of hunger, which must be appeased else nature revolts. The dark outcome of such starvation is the dreaded symptom of masturbation, or worse; and the harmony of society is seen to fall before an unrestrained and maniacal fury created by the individual's own solitude. The sexual passions are present in all creatures and yet they must only be engaged in once the physical body has grown enough to invest in them. The easiest and most celebrated way to appease this appetite is to marry, whereby you will furnish yourself with a mate for life and an equal partner for the resolving of your shared animal passions. Speaking from the practice of **physiology**, the right age to marry is known to be anytime after full puberty and only when there is felt to be a strong mutual attachment on both sides. Men generally desire to marry when they feel themselves to be men; women always as soon as they have become women.

Male Organs: - the biggest difference between the organs of generation of a man, and those of a woman, is that the man's are all external to the body. They are his *penis* and the *testicles,* the latter being importantly pouched in the *scrotum*. The penis is used for both copulation and urination, although not simultaneously. The production of seminal fluid is continual, although its discharge is intermittent. At that time, the penis, subject to sexual excitement, will swell with blood and distend, producing an erection.

The Female Organs: - the *ovaries, uterus* or *womb,* and *vagina* are the woman's internal organs and are situated within her abdomen. Her external organ is the *vulva* or *pudenda,* which is divided into two main parts; the *labia majora,* which is in two folds, and within these the *labia minora.* Situated inside the labia majora, and just above the labia minora, is the *clitoris.* These are the most sensitive of organs and the main seat of sexual sensation for a woman. Just below them is the opening to the vagina, which in virgins will often be guarded by a thin membrane known as the *hymen.* This is not always to be relied upon as a test of virginity as it can be destroyed by disease or accident, and in some cases has even been found to exist after the woman has gone through childbirth.

The Act of Union: - sexual congress, also known as the act of generation, the marital union, coitus or copulation, is accompanied by a nervous spasm which has been created by the excitement of the special nerves located on the man's penis and the woman's clitoris. The reaction is more exhausting to the human system than any other physical sensation it will encounter.

A Few Words on Puberty: -
Sexual love, although felt and acknowledged by the sexual organs, is based within the cerebral faculty. It can be cultivated or restrained the same as any other aspect of one's character. In children, especially during the trials of puberty, it must not be snubbed or repressed. In cases where this has occurred it has often been from a false delicacy on the part of the parents. All that is commonly required is to make certain that proper attention is paid to diet and general habits. This will ensure that a proper and healthy change from child to adult is achieved. Certain circumstances have been known to require more

rigorous attention to sexual morals. I have even heard that in 1859, in the lace factories of Nottingham, sexual intercourse occurs amongst boys and girls as young as 15, and even at that age they are frequently found to be suffering from venereal diseases. This is due in the most part to the unhealthily late hours the young threaders and winders are forced to keep, which lead to idle and irregular habits as they are often unoccupied during the daylight hours. This would be rectified with the proper attention to education and contraception.

Menstruation:-

It is the female child who will undergo the most dramatic of changes during puberty as her body adjusts to that of her womanly adult life. Several marked alterations will appear in her development and disposition. Most clearly displayed will be those of her bust, and the whole body and limbs will begin to assume a more rounded and shapely form so admired by the artists of our day. She will also undergo a change within her womb, as it prepares itself for when she will wish to bear children. This can be a most surprising change for a young girl, although occurring in the majority of women. Puberty is the herald of menstruation and first takes place in young ladies between the ages of 13 and 15. I have to say, it is well to bear in mind that it may be delayed somewhat, as its first occurrence depends very much on the yearly climate. In very hot climates girls are known to menstruate as young as ten years of age, whilst in colder climates it will be much later. As a rule, when the menses – as they can be known – appear at a younger age than usual they are known to disappear much earlier. This time of disappearance is known as the menopause or 'Change in Life'; in our part of the world this happens between 44 and 50 years of age.

Let me explain to you the origins of the word 'menstruation'. It is taken from the Latin *mensis*, meaning a month, and it is the medical name given to the flow experienced by women roughly once every month. I have been informed that it is perhaps better known to all concerned as the 'monthlies' or 'periods'. Women are most often in the habit of saying that they are merely 'unwell' whenever the flow appears. At first thought, the sufferers of this monthly illness do seem to fall victim to a state of life that is a hidden weight in the balance of the sexes; it seems to be both one-sided and useless. There has been no more common wail that echoes from the female sex than the cry of, '*Why on earth were we made such creatures?*' Or, more often, there are those who ask, '*What is the meaning of all this suffering and inconvenience?*' In answer, I can offer both reassurance and an explanation to those in need: -

The discharge that occurs is a shedding of the mucous membrane of the womb. This internal lining, which often appears as a small amount of debris, is mixed amongst the most obvious sign of the 'monthlies', the blood. Within this mixed discharge there will be found the ovum, without which pregnancy cannot occur. This monthly event naturally reoccurs for two reasons: -

1. The womb is constructed so that it must repeatedly cleanse and repair itself. This allows it to become fit and ready to receive the material produced by a man which is vital to the successful continuation of the species.

2. Each ovary – of which there are two, situated as a kind of wing flanking each side of the womb – operates under a synchronous natural monthly urge, which passes an ovum into the womb each month before the discharge occurs.

The 'monthlies' will most commonly last from two to eight days and are equal in weight to about two to eight ounces. Any abnormalities in this would lead me to believe that there is some other underlying illness from which the woman is suffering and which should be investigated by her doctor. Equally, a woman should seek medical aid if her monthly is accompanied by any pain.

Menstruation is therefore very wonderful, and having opened the door onto the secret world of the feminine sex, I am in no doubt that you will agree with me that it presents a most interesting series of phenomena for study for all those of a scientific mind.

Sexual Love and the Young: -
With the onslaught of puberty, the passionate emotions of sexual love begin to be expressed. I most forcefully suggest to you that the young MUST be taught to understand it – it is only the senseless and frequently cruel and destructive force of prudery on the part of the parents that withholds such knowledge from their offspring. It is the most natural of all desires. As a medical man myself, I can see no benefit in not adeptly educating your offspring in the matters concerning their own physical and mental natures. Learn from the dangers of the aforementioned lace factories in Nottingham! Beware of the peril of moral education being passed from schoolboy to schoolboy!

Has not the law only recently been changed to protect the young from unwise sexual conduct before a suitable age? The Select Committee of the House of Lords, first appointed in 1881 '*to inquire into the state of law relative to the protection of young girls from artifices to induce them to lead a corrupt life*'

'The Four Seasons of Life: Youth "The Season of Love"',
by F.F. Palmer and J. Cameron, c.1868, (Library of Congress).

has just published the following recommendation to raise the age of allowed carnal knowledge from 13 to 16. It does not favour you to indulge in the belief that sexual love waits until the marriage day to appear. The age at which it becomes possible comes with the complete physiological change experienced by both boy and girl; as I have stated earlier, the arrival of such changes vary according to climate, constitutions and the habits of life.

In the hottest of latitudes, the development can be both swift and early. In cooler, northern latitudes, it is slow, like the vegetation. In towns and cities I can most certainly attest it comes more rapidly than in the country and the risks of a stimulating diet will see it develop far more rapidly than a cooling one. Remember this in your dealings with your children. Do not shirk from the duty of installing within them that knowledge necessary for a long, healthy and prosperous life.

Sexual Desire: -

Sexual love in men and women is most easily understood as 'Sexual Desire'. It is the driving passion behind the entire human race. It is felt by all in differing quantities – there are those to whom it is an extreme and those who feel it as a soft breeze on a summer's day. The Licentious Libertine or the Sentimental Prude are wholly incapable of feeling or understanding its power.

I know there are those who say that *'woman has but little sensual desire'*. I would argue that they are wrong in the worst and most base of ways. Women love with their whole and complete soul. To a woman love is life; to a man, love is the joy of life. If he suffers misfortune in love, it will only bruise the man, even though it may bruise him deeply. To a woman, it is the ruin of life and wrecks her happiness. So I would state without fear that women feel love, and sexual love, most keenly. Love in marriage, and the love required for the creation of children, is reliant on the existence of sexual love. If this is not capable of being expressed by both parties, how is mankind supposed to continue in its reproductive enterprise? Since love implies the presence of sexual desire it can only truly exist between those persons willingly committed to creating a family. When this condition is found to be wanting, or is destroyed, then that love will be replaced by friendship.

The Invariable Risks of Celibacy: -

There are those who do not believe that sexual desire, or the love felt between a man and a woman, is worthy of their attention. I have attended meetings to hear them speak, those paragons of virtue, encapsulated – it has been reported – by a 'Dr.' Henry Philpot, a supposed leading light in the 'New Celibacy' movement. Their followers are encouraged to pledge themselves to *'eschew the joys and sorrows of matrimony'* and spend their lives devoted to intellectual pursuits so as to *'guide the thought of the world'*. I would remind the bachelors of England of the motto of one of our greatest and most noble leaders, the gallant Nelson, *'England expects every young man to do his duty'*.

The reported medical risks of celibacy are far too great to be ignored. In either sex, there can be no doubt that the celibate life creates the most miserable perversions of the mind and body. In men, I have seen the symptoms of mania, apoplexy and melancholy most clearly manifested. Other fearsome characteristics include a loss of vision, deafness and many various foul diseases of the skin. It is true, as well, I would not doubt that you are aware, that man's commitment to the celibate life is not so often strictly observed.

Should a man find he is denied the opportunity for sexual intercourse then there is a great risk of him turning to that most distressing of all practices,

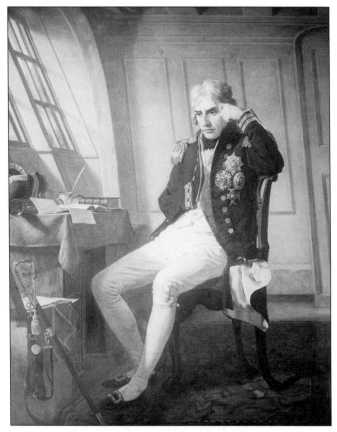

Lord Nelson in the cabin of the Victory,
by Charles Lucy 1814-1873, (Library of Congress).

masturbation. I shall say more on this matter later, for it is deserving of special attention. Whilst it has the sole benefit of warding off the evils that I have previously listed in great measure, it allows a number of far worse such terrors to appear in their place. In women, celibacy, which society prizes as the highest and most brilliant quality for her to possess, can – in certain cases and with little provocation – sadly submit her to the horrors of hysteria and other such nervous derangements. The only recommendation I can support for the course of celibacy is for those unfortunate peoples who have been born carrying the marks of the polluted disease of syphilis. Although their crime is an innocent one – the guilt resting heavily on the souls of their parents – it is inadvisable for them to seek a match or physical union and pass the pollution on to their lover. Let them be content with the bonds of friendship.

The simple joining of two compatible souls in the bond of marriage will allay any fears resulting from celibacy; and to the Bachelors and Maids of England I would have one final motto to give on this important matter, Choose Love, Choose Life.

The Marriage Age: -

'When does it arrive?' I hear you cry. The medical answer is that it depends very much upon solar heat. In those hot latitudes of which I have already spoken, and where the young are believed to develop quickly – again, like the vegetation – boys reportedly become husbands at the age of 14, and girls become wives as young as 12. This is somewhat shocking to our ears, after our own battles on the age of sexual maturity, but such cultural differences come with our ever-expanding Empire.

In England, happily, the marrying age depends on two certain things: if there is money enough to provide and if there is a suitable lover. In medical opinion the age of this causes some argument. One voice claims that this may range anywhere from a woman who has turned 16 until she has reached the age of 40; for a man, it will be from the age of 18 until he feels he is ready to make his will. Other voices, and more numerous and vocal in their conviction, say that neither man nor woman should marry till the physical powers of the whole body have most fully developed. For a man this will be seen between the ages of 23 and 26, for a woman it is 18 to 21. I favour the latter opinion.

One final word on when to marry, if you will allow me to further indulge. Permitted and sanctioned by social usage and our current laws, the marriage of first cousins is often seen in our society, but it has disastrous consequences for the health of all parties concerned. Great families who intermarry, believing it will preserve their wealth or maintain their titles, have been seen to follow the path of invariable decay, leading only to their extinction.

The Practice of Physiognomy: -

It is not difficult, even in our modern world, to see the relics of simpler times. Fortune-telling was often a relied-upon practice for those seeking advice on the right circumstances to find a proper mate. Self-constituted oracles loudly claimed the ability to offer prophetic glimpses into the future with a 'science' based on a limited understanding of the applicants. Although still a common sight today, they are under threat from that most practical of sciences:

Physiognomy.

Although this wonderful art has its detractors, its practitioners should be shown

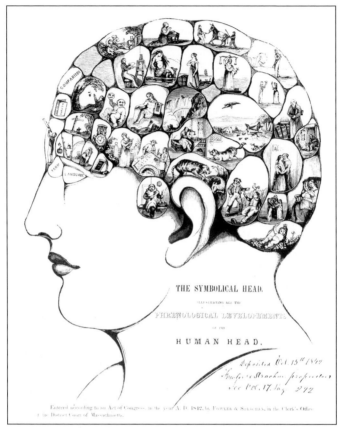

THE SYMBOLICAL HEAD.

PHRENOLOGICAL DEVELOPMENTS

HUMAN HEAD.

The Symbolical head, illustrating all the phrenological
developments of the human head, c. 1842, (Library of Congress).

the same degree of respect as those marvellous individuals engaged in the study
of **Phrenology**. I am an avid supporter of both Physiognomists and
Phrenologists, the first being designed to identify the workings of the inner
mind of man from his outer form, and the second being the focus of careful
cranial observations of the human head to divine internal character.

Both these practices have been refined, through rigorous observation and
analysis, into a most beneficial and reliable modern science. Phrenology is
widely used to explore the criminal or racial characteristics of man and so I
think it regards little mention in the pursuit of marriage. Instead, I shall discuss
the solid and educational advice that can be obtained from a clear
understanding of the physiognomic discipline. The publication in 1881 of
Mary Olmstead Stanton's *Physiognomy. A Practical and Scientific Treatise,* a

book which has garnered reviews in the newspapers, was written with the authoress's belief that '*Man's knowledge of himself seems not to have kept pace with the knowledge of his surroundings*'.

To know oneself, as much to know another, is a great advantage in the practical application of physiognomy. It is one of the most essential sciences, which can be used by the most non-scientific individual to obtain for oneself a deep understanding and knowledge of mankind and, most importantly, it can furnish you with information about how to make a proper match that will guarantee healthy and vigorous children.

One of the tenets of Physiognomy is the importance of bodily harmony.

'*Mating Time*' by Gordon Ross for *Puck Magazine*, early 1900s, (Library of Congress).

The suitability of two individuals who will be physically joined together, the elements of masculine and feminine, positive and negative, in a singular act. As those elements are different from one another, so 'bodily harmony' means the joining of physical opposites. I have seen this most clearly in the union of dark and light persons; fleshy and lean; big boned and slightly built; and tall and short.

I would further still advise those of a dark-haired complexion to always marry those who are lighter than themselves. Light should marry dark, and those predisposed to flesh from indulgence should marry those who are lucky to find their constitution to be lean. It is the easiest practice to apply, as a simple understanding of physical difference is clear to any person in possession of good eyesight. But there is not only a scientific advantage to choosing a lover who contrasts to yourself, as this blending of two persons of opposite body shapes is commonly believed to produce an experience that our greatest poets have referred to as '*the union of a soul within a soul*'.

But what do these physical characteristics tell us about the internal workings of the person you might choose to be your husband or wife? I have devised a simple guide – usually on sale at a reasonable price – which will present the most important physical markers for the character of man: -

Round or Plump Form: - men and women of this bodily shape are commonly seen to take the world on with an easy and affable nature. They are fond of good living and pleasure. Amongst women, they are always known to be the best cooks, and both sexes usually show great enjoyment in trade, finding themselves easily adaptable to the variations or changes of both business and life that generally befall them. Above all else, they require good feeding, are jolly as long as their personal comforts are seen to be attended to, and they are not likely to be the strictest when it comes to the attendance of religious duties.

Sharp and Angular Form: - husbands and wives of this shape are the reverse of the round and the plump, but do not judge them unfavourably! They are found to be energetic and often in earnest. They will strive and push those around them, they may find fault and worry about the laziness of others. Often I have seen them to be progressive and thoughtful, but caring little for the pleasures of life indulged in by the ordinary man. As husbands they can be both kind and thoughtful, although there is a danger of them turning very obstinate, refusing to concede in an argument, and often are at their least amiable when subjected to a wife who is nagging or one who has neglected her perceived duties. As wives, sharp and angular women are often industrious and quite able to manage the tasks life may set them. They have been described as 'peppery-tempered', and do not suffer fools – or idle husbands.

Tall and Short: - persons who are tall in stature exhibit the greatest amount of self-control. They are renowned for their calm temperament, less given to uncontrolled excitability, make few mistakes from decisions based on impulse and are far more deliberate in their choices. Short people exhibit the opposite of all these characteristics. It is widely agreed that riotous mobs are always composed of rather short people. The tall fine-bodied person is the ideal specimen of coolness and this should be remembered by those fiery-tempered short men as a tall wife would be more likely to gently soothe their troubled spirits than they are to decide to smash all their china.

On Foot Size: - one of the most favourable indicators of an individual's character will be the size of their feet. Big-footed men and women may seem awkward on the first meeting, but they are the most reliable and steady of partners. Small-footed persons are dangerously prone to gaiety and evolutions across the ballroom.

The Shape of the Neck: - those in possession of a thick short neck are often acknowledged as the most obstinate, exacting and selfish of persons. The most extreme form will always be found in the male sex, who is given to treating their wives as lowly servants, and, akin to Henry the Eighth, regard a wife's obedience to be her highest virtue. They can be sagacious and shrewd and are advised to avoid alcohol as they can become somewhat liberal after dinner. A small long neck is more commonly found in women than it is in men, and has generally been taken to indicate some form of physical weakness. They will not make ardent lovers and are commonly far more amiable and affectionate than given to passionate embracing, but fond of innocent caressing. They are renowned for being utterly deficient of any animal selfishness.

The Shape of the Chin: - taken to be a sign of physical endurance, the broad and square chin can also denote an underlying disposition of a jealous and exacting nature. A person in possession of this shape of chin will favour being waited on by others. They are often dogged and pertinacious in company and to some, they may be known as a good friend, but beware for they make the most bitter enemy. Conversely, those of a long chin or nose have an ample supply of grace and humility.

The Shape of the Lips: - if you wish to find someone who will demonstrate an ardent and loving disposition, look for those with full and prominent lips. They will have a fondness for kissing, although are also liable to form an attachment and fall in love too quickly. They will also have a long and tender regard for children. Thin-lipped people are often found to be less loving as husbands and wives, and frequently far less forgiving. Those possessed of a small mouth will be orderly, and most commonly precise in all little things they undertake. When angry they are the most likely to be sarcastic and cutting towards their adversary.

The Mouth: - the mouth that turns upwards at the outermost corners reveals a character who seeks fun and mischief in all things. Those with an upturned mouth will never break their heart for love and in either sex the wearer is gifted with a unique talent for flirtation. They are not averse to engaging in a little harmless deception and will always be found to be the most merry and pleasant of persons. But a mouth where the outermost corners are clearly turned down is the mouth belonging to those regularly given to obstinacy and sullenness. They may be companionable when pleased, but generally sedate or grim in nature and only given to public amicability under the strictest protest. If your lover is in possession of a well-formed mouth, which runs as near as possible to a straight line, this counts most heavily in their favour. A harmonious character will always be demonstrated in the clear depiction of well-formed physical features.

A Note on Noses: - I would advise you that no man should attempt to marry a woman with a nose that is similar to his own – their household will be a constant battleground. Many of the women who are gifted with a Roman nose should not attempt to marry at all, or if they choose to, they must make sure to find a small-nosed submissive husband – none other will be desirable.

Dr. Dimmick's Anatomy of the Human Body

For those who wish to obtain the greater understanding of the practice of physiognomy, you would do well to invest in the latest edition of the most brilliant work written by Dr. J. Simms M.D. Previously published in the United States of America in 1879, *Nature's Revelations of Character; or, Physiognomy Illustrated. A description of the Mental, Moral and Volitive dispositions of mankind, as manifested in the human form and countenance* contains 260 engravings on all aspects of human nature that can be read in the human form. It is available under the simpler title of *Revelations of Character* from the publisher William Tweedie, 337 Strand, London, priced at 21 shillings.

It is clear that physiognomy contains within it the information most beneficial to the scientific and medical deductions used to choose one's lover. As a man of both science and medicine I cannot ignore the valuable advice that can be easily collected by even the most casual of students. There are, however, certain characteristics that defy scientific understanding. It is a well-known fact, although one with little medical reasoning, that the female heart will always show a weakness towards military uniforms. I have been told that it is the cavalryman who maintains a woman's preference. Another, and happily less combative external attraction, is to be found in that emblem of virility, the secondary – but publicly viewable – symbol of your generative power: The Beard. Just as women will bestow a special cultivation and dressing of their hair, men who seek to please and attract women must take care to cultivate not just a most elegant growth of beard, but most importantly, a moustache.

Masculine Women and Effeminate Men: -

A short note here on the subject of masculine and feminine, its relation to the sexes, and the attributes and characteristics belonging to each sex. This is a subject greatly debated by medical men and poets alike. There are those who say that the masculine woman *'brings discredit on the girls of to-day'*. She is warned that characteristics that are too male – athletic prowess; cigarette smoking; slang-speaking and masculine dress – will lose her the respect, nay worse, the reverence toward chivalrous treatment that every right-minded man owes to a 'true' woman. They warn that a horsey young lady, with a loud voice and a strident laugh, is the epitome of undesirable unwomanliness. I recently heard the tale of a young lady, known as one of the 'New Women', who, once married, continually quoted Goethe's apothegm: *Was uns alle badigt, das Gemeine* – translated as 'That which keeps us all in bondage, the commonplace' – and used a pistol to summon her servants. How dangerously unfeminine this 'New Woman' appears to be! But what of her male counterparts, those men who are as feminine as she is masculine – what of them?

Illustrated Police News, 20 July 1895.

It seems a symptom of our age to view those men who are feminine in character as dangerous and pass it in conversation from one to another that they shall be disliked by women and that those women who contain more than a generous amount of the masculine element will only ever be capable of finding favour with the effeminate men. Turning to the *Huddersfield Chronicle* in 1893 I found this most interesting article on the subject: -

Effeminate men, according to a writer in **Hearth and Home**, *are becoming objectionably prominent in London, and by these signs is the effeminate man to be known. He has a thin, high-pitched voice, and very white hands, 'which he is fond of flourishing about'. He often clasps bangles around his wrists, walks out in open-work stockings and gloves with a dozen buttons, and laces or straps himself in that his waist may be visible to the naked eye. Moreover, continues this unsparing critic, 'it is an absolute fact that a large number of young men get themselves up. The rouge-pot and the powder-puff find a place* *upon their toilet table; their hair is often crimped or curled, and sometimes even dyed; and their figures are trained and artificially improve. Will society tolerate these beings' asks the writer; and the answer is obviously – Yes; equally with the masculine woman.*

A well respected author once told me, '*The more completely masculine a man is, the more manly and the more loveable he is to woman; and the more truly effeminate woman, be she plain or beautiful, will find getting a lover not difficult.*' Complementary to the physical characteristics, a person must also have the right blend of masculine or feminine mental characteristics otherwise they will find no success in the art of love. It was reported to me at a recent medical seminar that a man afforded great pleasure to the art of 'winning' a woman, seeing her as a country to be conquered.

In the union of love, a modest woman who makes sure to keep her lover at bay and herself on the defensive until the final moment of surrender, is an action of great psychological importance. In everyday life man is in a constant battle against the obstacles he meets and so he must firmly overcome them. Nature has given him a more aggressive character than that of a woman, far more of the masculine element than she normally possesses, to guarantee his success in this task. So a modern woman, who uses her modesty and her femininity to ensure that he feels she must be conquered, makes certain that this most natural reaction is observed. I left the seminar unconvinced, although the idea was clearly supported by those around me.

Masturbation: -
Whilst the sexual organs are capable of doing great work, their desires are equally capable of inflicting severe harm on a person's moral fibre. Libertinism, in whatever manner it is practised, whether by solitary indulgence or excessive venery with other individuals, will always be found to be most hurtful and destructive to life. The disease of onanism – as masturbation is known – amongst men has received widespread medical analysis since the eighteenth century, but few authors have discussed the prevalence of the act amongst both boys *and* girls. I am happy to report the most well-known authority on this subject is J.H. Kellogg, the American inventor of the Kellogg's Corn Flake Cereal which is designed for those in need of an unstimulating diet. In 1888 he published *Treatment for Self-Abuse and its Effects: Plain Facts for Old and Young,* which has dealt most deeply with this vice and its dangers for both sexes. It is a universally occurring fetish, emerging with the onslaught of puberty. Its practitioners can be of any age, both old and young. It has many

other names: self-pollution, self-abuse and the solitary or Secret Vice. There are no bounds to its indulgence and I have read of one individual indulging in it up to seven or eight times a day which significantly reduced both his mental and physical faculties.

But how does it come about? There are many physical causes – constipation, piles, irritable bladder, local uncleanliness, and sleeping on feather beds will often produce the habit in both males and females. Certain types of exercise, such as climbing or lying upon one's back or abdomen can provoke sexual excitement which will lead to self-abuse. And it has been claimed that some occasionally experience sexual desire after whipping – which I would severely discourage as a childhood punishment given this risk. Dietary stimulation is another cause of the vice – tea, coffee, tobacco, candies, cinnamon, cloves, many spices, peppermint and other strong essences are known to be powerful exciters of the genitals, and must be avoided. Mustard, pepper, rich-gravies, beer, wine, hard cider and tobacco will all create a craving for sensual gratification. They should be avoided at all costs.

There are also numerous social causes that can be linked to the widespread occurrence of this polluting vice. For young women, there are certain causes that will always lead to the formation of this most evil of habits. A Vicious Companion, who becomes dearer to the girl than her own mother and whose counsel she turns to above all others, is in the most dangerous position to lead an innocent girl astray. One must be sure to avoid forming attachments to girls who are vain, silly or idle, or who are rude in their manners and irreverent and disobedient to parents and teachers. Such a girl should be shunned.

Another cause is as treacherous as liquor or opium, and that is the reading of Sentimental Books. Their influence upon the mind is highly damaging, exciting the emotions and heightening internal passions which are then only gratified by the self-abuse. Finally, there can be no greater warning than against an overfamiliarity with the opposite sex. Girls are prone to encouraging silly letters from the boys and young men of their acquaintance to whom they will also often write in return. These childish flirtations must be immediately discouraged as they will only lead to those evils of a most revolting character.

As with young women, young men must also avoid Bad Company, Bad Books and Bad Language. Equally horrifying is the influence of Vile Pictures, calculated to inflame the passions and lead to Evil Thoughts and Vice. Thousands of these pictures are in circulation across the country through agents whose sole mission is to encourage this vice and lead to the destruction of numerous young men. It was not until 1857 and the passing of Lord

Campbell's Act against Obscene Publications that the law sought to restrict this damaging and immoral industry.

The effects resulting from the Secret Vice are clearly evident in even the most mild of cases and are impossible to disguise. Weariness; coughing; defective development; a sudden change in disposition; irritability; idleness; a dull and vacant expression; sleeplessness; forgetfulness; fickleness; untrustworthiness; a new love of solitude; bashfulness or an unnatural boldness; a capricious appetite and craving of clay, slate pencils, plaster or chalk; an unnatural paleness; acne or pimples; biting of the fingernails; and wetting of the bed are all indicators of indulgence in self-pollution.

Physical symptoms in the man include pain or irritation in his genital organs, kidneys or bladder. Other general effects include: nervous exhaustion; a general debilitation; consumption; dyspepsia; heart disease; afflictions of the throat; nervous diseases; epilepsy; deafness; dimness of vision; headache; a weak back; pains in the limbs and a stiffness in the joints; paralysis; irregular flushing of the face; irritation of the spinal cord; and insanity. In women, the vice will, of course, produce different reactions, although some symptoms are shared.

The secretions from the vagina will produce a soreness in the roots of the nails on the fingers, which will be accompanied by warts in the same area, a clear sign of pollution. It will cause menstrual irregularities; cancer of the womb; sterility; shrivelling of the breasts or a lack of development; *pruritis* – a terrible itching of the genitals – which can reduce its sufferer to a state of acute frenzy; and an inability to resist the manipulation of the genitals, even in the presence of strangers or relatives. In cases of this extremis, amputation of the part is often found to be the only cure. Insanity, spinal irritation, nervous exhaustion and nervous diseases are far more pronounced in women than in men, and it is the most common cause of that dreaded of diseases – *Hysteria*.

For men, the nocturnal emissions, which occur during sleep, are just as dangerous as the waking act, and are often accompanied by erotic dreams. This nocturnal pollution is referred to as *spermatorrhoea* and is often found in those attempting to reform from a previously lascivious path. The immediate effect at the morning discovery of such emissions is one of melancholy, which can lead to despair and even suicide.

When masturbation has been indulged in to great excess on the part of a woman, the clitoris will always lose its sensitivity, though in some cases it has been known to become hypersensitive and most discomforting. It will alter in appearance, becoming elongated and will hang down. The labia majora and the whole entrance to the vagina will be seen to be an intensely coloured red and congested, with all parts covered in a profuse secretion of mucus. The labia minora will also be elongated and pulled outwards, and I have seen cases in hospital where this condition is so bad that they resemble the ears of a spaniel. For a man the visual physical effect on his sexual organs is a thinning and shrinking of his penis, which will be cold to the touch at multiple points along the main trunk.

Disease: -

Diseases of the sexual organs are the most terrible and lasting in nature. Not only do they indicate a pollution of the body, but many are the result of the pollution of the soul. I will set out those diseases of which we are most at risk in our modern society in the hope it will better equip those parties who will need to secure themselves against infection. For a greater understanding of the treatments available to you, please refer to the later volume written by my colleague, Mr. Mandrake.

The symptoms of masturbation I have discussed in great detail, so I will restrict myself merely to a discussion of its treatment and cure. The first method must be one of prevention of the habit; education of the children; and a steely resolve on the part of the adult not to indulge in the practice. Daily exercise should be taken to the extent of fatigue, or the cultivation of an interest in botany, geology or entomology should be encouraged. Collecting specimens of natural history is the most welcome diversion and one that encompasses both the physical and mental faculties. Solitude on these activities must be avoided at all costs and so the enlisting of a cheerful companion to accompany the patient should always be encouraged. The science of **physiology**, close to those celebrated fields of physiognomy and phrenology, teaches us that our thoughts are governed by what we eat. Precautions for diet should be followed thus: -

Never Overeat. Gluttony is fatal to chastity.

Eat But Twice A Day. Nothing should be eaten within four or five hours of bedtime. If the stomach contains undigested food then the sleep will be disturbed and cause erotic dreams and nightmares.

Discard All Stimulating Food. Spices, pepper, ginger, mustard, cinnamon, cloves, essences, all condiments, salt pickles, animal food of all kinds including fish, fowl, oysters, eggs and milk. This may be hard for some, and to those I would allow a very little lean beef or mutton and a moderate use of milk and salt – the less the better.

Avoid Stimulating Drinks. Wine, beer, tea and coffee must be rejected in all circumstances. Chocolate should be discarded, tobacco and all hot drinks.

Eat Only: Fruits, grains and vegetables, with oatmeal and flour.

After diet, sleep is the most important method for controlling sexual excess. Required practice for all persons is an early night, which will give them seven to nine hours of restful sleep. Take a warm bath on rising, or sun baths with the help of electric baths, sprays or plunges.

But if these preventative methods have failed, I can suggest more forceful methods. A cool bath should be taken several times a day and most especially at night. Also to be applied at night, a beneficial wet compress pressed to the lower portion of the spine which will cool the heat held in the genital organs. Enemas should be used with caution, but can be beneficial in some cases. Electricity, most skilfully applied by a trusted agent, will accomplish more than any other method. The use of a metallic instrument will apply electricity to the point of greatest inflammation – do so for about 15 minutes and the patient should find relief for two to three weeks. Circumcision for male patients is of great relief for those suffering from an irritation of fluid. Any of the Drugs or Preventative Rings employed by men have a limited success.

I will now turn to that most debilitating disease, one that affects a large proportion of the individuals in our country, the horrors of *Hysteria*. From the oldest records of medical history, hysteria has been regarded as the suffering most acutely linked with the female sex. But modern science has discovered that the organs of generation in men can, in rare cases, also cause them to suffer from this disease. It must not be treated as a trivial matter, or one that is the result of a diseased imagination. It requires substantial and thorough treatment of both the mental and physical faculties. But the most common and successful cure for a sufferer of either sex is that of marriage, which relieves most of the symptoms of the disease other than in the most extreme cases.

There are those diseases which result from an infectious sexual connection. The worst form of venereal disease is the dreaded syphilis. Soon after

Face of a Syphilis Sufferer.
Artist: Steven Kirk.

infection, a very slight lesion, similar to a small boil, will appear near to the genital organs. This will rapidly infect the entire system and poison the whole body, for which there is no cure. In the most degraded and terminal forms its malignant ulceration destroys the organs of speech, penetrating deep into the skull even into the brain itself! Foul sores cover the entire body and often the nose, tongue, lips or an eye will rot clean away and yet the wretched sufferer lives on.

As a penalty against illicit sexual activity, nature has invented a safeguard in the form of the most loathsome and incurable diseases known to man. *Gonorrhoea*, although causing the person a great deal of suffering, is curable and will leave no trace of its infection. In certain cases however, it will leave a serious mutilation and infection of a person once will leave no immunity for them against further infection. In the most extreme cases it will result in a sudden loss of virile power and will produce a severe form of melancholia as a life without the fulfilment of love is seen by many as being a mere blank.

Mrs Dollymop's Advice for the Single Woman

On Womanhood – The Importance of Being Yourself – Hair, Make-up, and Perfume – The Padded Bust – Health and Fashion – The Monthlies – Flirtation – When to Marry – Choosing a Husband – The Wedding Day – Women to Admire

Ladies, the modern world is, at times, a befuddling place to navigate. Herein I will guide you through the main attributes of femininity, from costume and dress to the many ideas of womanliness and the art of securing a husband. I will end my ruminations with a list of women for whom there is no equal, no muse greater, no voice clearer, than theirs who have been known as 'woman' during our glorious time. But before we begin, the essay below, written in 1877, is for your rumination so that you can better understand the complexities of 'womanhood' in our age.

Last evening the Rev. Eli Fay, minister of the Upper Chapel, Norfolk-street, delivered the first of a series of lectures he intends to give on 'Woman.' The particular subject of last night's discourse was 'Woman in the Realm of Thought,' and Mr. Fay, who is from America, sought to show that woman, although essentially different from man, is in no way his inferior.

Opening with the words of Genesis, 1st Chapter 27th verse, the rev. gentleman said there was an ineradicable difference between man and woman, a difference in structure, and a difference intellectually and physically. Nor did the fact that there were women like Cornelia, Joan of Arc, Miss Nightingale, and Mrs. Beecher Stowe to place against Cromwell and Napoleon, Michaelangelo, Shakespeare, and Beethoven, alter this fact. The mind of Mrs. Stowe, while the clearest, strongest, and best balanced in the Beecher family, was yet essentially a female mind. Feminine men and masculine women were monstrosities, and any attempt to repress the characteristics of either sex by education was against the law of nature. Man was granite, woman was Italian marble.

But still it did not follow that woman was inferior to man; there were far more suicides among men than among women – while a man committed suicide a woman wept and died at her post. Woman had no more difficulty than Man in mastering the sciences and practical matters. Madam de Stael was a power among the French diplomatists, and our own Queen Victoria was said to hold very decided opinions on public matters. Still statesmanship was not the sphere of woman.

The reverend gentleman then condemned and deplored the unjust discrimination which excluded the sex from our great seats of learning, and pointed out that the intellect of woman had not been found wanting in any department in which it had been tried. To say that woman was inferior was an insult to our wives and sisters, and he urged that the sex should have an opportunity of displaying their capacity.

While man's education continued for years after woman's, indeed during his life, she when she married settled down to the treadmill of domestic duties, and often actually retrograded in knowledge. He believed that the domestic duties of woman were a sacred mission, but he urged that husbands should encourage their wives, who were almost always their best counsellors, to take an interest in what was going on in the world, and not encourage them to lavish their time on idle vanities. The intellectual progress of women often ended on their wedding-day, and they were not nearly so bright at 40 as at 20.

Mr. Fay then enumerated the causes which circumcised the realm of thought in women, and declared that if women were allowed fair opportunities for education they would often prove better help-mates than now. Women too often gave themselves up to dress and idle dissipation, and who were *responsible but the men who preferred a pretty face and attractive person to rare intellectual and moral worth in plain attire.*

The Importance of Being Yourself: -

I admire beauty in a woman, but what I have grown to admire more in all my days of schooling is sound common sense, and this is true of all the best society. *Unless a beautiful woman is possessed of this sterling quality her beauty indeed falls flat upon us.* A woman – as much as a man – must attend to her health; we have a right to possess just as good health, and perhaps better. All women would be healthier and nonetheless beautiful if they are in the possession of firm muscles and strong limbs. Often, young women are given to comparing themselves to

Lithograph by Currier & Ives, c.1870, (Library of Congress).

popular ideas of beauty, or, far more serious in nature, against the characteristics of their friends.

To those young women I would say this, '*Notions concerning beauty are almost as varied as human features: what will be attractive to one may be absurd to another.*' Above all else, it is as Shakespeare himself once wrote, when attending to matters of love and beauty: '*This above all – To thine own self be true; And must it follow, as the night follows the day, Thou canst not then be false to any man.*'

Hair, Make-up, and Perfume: -

Whilst there can be no greater mark of a woman's character than the acknowledgement of her truthful and gentle nature, there are few who would claim that they do not walk this earth without the added artifice of being made up in some way or another. *Young and old, savage and civilized, all try either to improve natural defects or acquired flaws.* Those who are blessed with a pretty face will always believe that they must polish, and even those of the more mature years are given to seeking out those methods for the removal of crow's feet. *All do something.* Should you too feel the need for such devices, remember that none of them should be used without the personal recommendation of trusted friends – never rely on that which has been printed or advertised and certainly don't be led away by the claims of 'Thousands of Testimonials' as so often seen in the pages of the newspapers or in shop windows. These are merely there to fool unsuspecting young women into spending money they wouldn't usually be inclined to spend.

There is a myriad of ways the young woman may alter her appearance to further beautify herself in this most modern of centuries. Lotions, enamels, roughing compounds, skin tighteners, powders and ointments are the kinds of items chiefly utilised and equally abused, successfully and otherwise, for the bare skin surface. Fakery is seen in abundance, from paddings, bustles, wigs, eyes and teeth, and in the most unfortunate of cases, even noses and ears have been provided to replace articles that have been lost or removed. These can be of such an artistic moulding and accuracy of outline that they would happily do credit to the best of sculptors. Although if badly done they will look most frightful and disturbing to the eye.

Should women everywhere practise the art of 'Make-up'? Most certainly they should! It is the duty of every living being to make the best of his or her appearance, whatever it is that they imagine the best to entail, for the sake of society and the universal pleasure of seeing beautiful things wherever you turn. It may be of interest to the casual observer that there are only two penetrations of the flesh which are done for beauty's sake in our country today: ear-piercing for the wearing of rings and the tattooing of the skin. I have left out any surgical plastic operations as these are done for medical benefits rather than for beauty's sake alone.

The most usual act of 'making-up' for a woman is the dyeing of her hair. *Almost every colour in the rainbow can be produced by dyes if necessary, but black, golden, light brown or brown are the ones most commonly chosen.* This is a practised art and it is best to seek professional aid in the matter as to attempt hair dyeing in the domestic setting may often lead to misadventure – although professional attendance will not always guarantee your safety. It might appear as though it has done its wonderful work to perfection when you are viewing it in the looking glass, but to the eyes of others it may look positively atrocious – there is the danger of giving yourself far too much of a golden hue, which will look unnatural, and your eyes will miss those undyed roots left on the side of the head which will so easily and often be seen by others. So the domestic hair-dye enthusiast must take special care to get at the hair roots and not miss those little bits in front of the ears. Then you will have achieved perfection and brought a delicate improvement to your natural features.

A brief warning on the practice of dyeing: it is common knowledge that fatalities have occurred through the application of hairdressing. Who has not heard of the sad death of a lady whose hair caught fire whilst being dressed in a fashionable West End shop? Let this be a warning to every student of the art of self making-up. Mind that the general health is not injured and be careful to see that the skin is not damaged nor the hair be made to come off by the use of advertised and fraudulent compounds.

'*The face is the region of the body that lends itself most kindly to the artistic advantages of "Touching Up". A little rouge, enamel, or powder – and there you are! Some pencilling to the eyebrows and darkening stuff for the lids and there it comes! Beauty out of plainness. The thing is so easy.*' So speaks many a great authority on the art of 'make-up'. But it must always be remembered that this can be a somewhat dangerous practice morally, as well as physically, for there are certain women who are well noted for their practice of making-up and who are often recognised for their lascivious livelihood by their powdered face alone. A respectable woman must take care that her roughing and dyeing, enamelling and padding, is at all time discreet and always in addition to the observance of scrupulous manners, lest she be mistaken for a fast and immoral woman. '*Touching up' the face must be done thoroughly well, or not at all.*

A final note on the use of perfumes. This is a somewhat vexing issue; some women utterly believe in their use, others cannot bear them. Should perfumes be used? I would answer both yes and no. If they are used to disguise an odour which cannot be got rid of by ordinary means, then they are certainly justifiable.

The Padded Bust: -

Of all the sections of the anatomy that a woman has at her disposal to demonstrate her feminine nature, the bust is the one of the most important for her to pay attention to. There are those who are sadly afflicted with a deficiency of nature's fullness and they must seek the substance of their silhouette from some other means. Again, here I must offer a warning against certain lotions or drugs that are advertised to restore '*that natural profile so desirable to the sex*'. No good can come of such methods, regardless of the claims of advertising and such quack productions are only in existence because the defrauded purchaser dare not complain as it might bring down some ridicule upon her.

Glamour photograph c. 1899, (Library of Congress).

The only legitimate procedure to alter the figure is bust padding, though it must be said that it might be considered rather a cruel deception by some women and directed towards the other sex. In my mind, a good deal will depend upon the circumstances. All women must understand that when a man loves and admires his *fiancée* for her many good points, it will also be his idea of her beautiful figure that has been drawn from the silhouette she shows to him. He may be a little disappointed if he should find out on their wedding night that all this fine beauty has been paid for in Regent Street and only consists for the most part of cotton wool. However, in the case of those who suffer from deformities, such as a curved spine or rounded shoulders, any judicious or skilful padding will derive much benefit for the aid of your figure and this is understandable in all cases.

Health and Fashion: -

A word here on corsets, for it is not possible to be without one once you have achieved a mature age. There are many benefits in the wearing of a corset – posture, figure and frame are all pleasingly extenuated. But it is a device easily misused by those afflicted with an inflated sense of vanity. There are those who have conceived the idea that small waists are the be-all and end-all of a woman's beauty. These foolish creatures are so consumed with the desire for a waist of minute proportions that they have injured themselves by sleeping in very tight corsets. The consequence of such a silly idea has been this: their general health has suffered severely and any other points of attractiveness have diminished just as they wished their waist to. HEALTH is much more beautiful. Do we not see this proved by the classical statues?

Lithograph by Currier & Ives, c.1856-1907 (Library of Congress).

It is a *moderately* small waist that should be desired, something that falls between a man's and a modiste's. There is nothing more valuable to a woman than her own good health; *without it, nobody is well off and nobody is really beautiful.* Any process a woman indulges in to improve herself which results in the infliction of injury to the skin or internal organs must be hunted out, exposed and held up as a strict warning to all in her acquaintance. For a time such improvements may be believed to be a success but later results, especially those that appear over time, must always be carefully taken into account. For instance, arsenic has been known to improve the appearance of the skin in some people, whilst in others it may produce quite the opposite effect.

There are some women who have sought to do away with the traditional costume of domestic femininity altogether and this is something about which I am somewhat at odds to counsel my younger readers. This 'New Woman' sees fit to dress as a man, walk as a man and live as a man, with a man's freedoms and expressions. I admire her vigour, but am not sure London is quite prepared to greet her, as this cutting from 1894 portrays:

> *London has treated to a glimpse of the 'New Woman,' who, in company with a gentleman friend, invaded Kew Gardens recently attired in a tweed Norfolk jacket, with knickerbockers and a straw boating hat. There is certainly no place in the wide world where the eccentricities of dress or deportment are less noticed than in the Metropolis, the peculiar charm of which, according to Mr. J. M. Barrie, is the fact that there, and only there, can a man eat a penny bun in the streets without anyone turning round to look at him. But in Kew Gardens it seems that even a 'New Woman' cannot wear knickerbockers without attracting attention, and that too, of a not altogether flattering description. At any rate, this was the experience of the lady alluded to, who, with her comrade, had to walk away very fast to escape being well-nigh mobbed by an audibly critical crowd.*

Illustrated Police News, 14 September 1895.

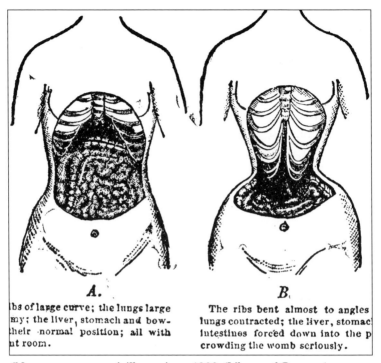

A.

bs of large curve; the lungs large
my; the liver, stomach and bow-
heir normal position; all with
t room.

B.

The ribs bent almost to angles
lungs contracted; the liver, stomac
Intestines forced down into the p
crowding the womb seriously.

'Nature versus corsets', illustration c.1903, (Library of Congress).

This is not a subject for polite conversation and best discussed in private with your doctor or mother. However, I will offer this small piece of advice: during the appearance of your monthlies, or 'turns' as some women are prone to calling them, make certain to avoid the following: - indigestible food, dancing in warm rooms, sudden exposure to cold or wet and mental agitations.

Flirtation: -

And so, having discussed the nature and practice of womanhood in its various forms, let us now turn to the practices and art of love. To begin, a warning: jealousy is an invariable attendant upon any courtship, for both sexes. Do not seek to inspire it in your lover as a game. It can be difficult for an inexperienced lover to tread the cautious line between flirtation and seduction, revealing their unwholesome lusts too soon before the marriage union allows. Ladies, remember that in all your conversations with men modesty is the most winning and womanly attribute to a woman's character, and this is shortly followed by that most desirable of qualities, *domesticity*. Both these qualities can be used to your advantage in the game of flirtation, but be careful not to appear either too reserved or too accessible. No man marries a woman of either extreme.

Do not fall hopelessly in love with the first man whose pays attention to you; there can be such a thing as a first, second and third loves, or loves successive and indefinite in number. But of all, it is True Love that is the most elusive and worth waiting for. Love is an intensifying of your ordinary life; love for a woman has no past, as it has no future, it merely IS. For a woman every love is a first love. Flirtation allows you to learn about love, and about the man who seeks an attachment to you, in a gentle way. But do not rely solely on it for your own purpose; it is not one thing, but the deft and artistic arrangement of many points of attraction that draws the fullest admiration of men. Flirtation allows you to request intimate questions with your beloved, a guide to which is offered below:

Fan Flirtation: -
Carrying right hand in front of face – *Follow me*.
Carrying in left hand – *Desirous of an acquaintance*.
Placing it on the right ear – *You have changed*.
Twirling it in left hand – *I wish to get rid of you*.
Drawing across the forehead – *We are watched*.
Carrying in right hand – *You are too willing*.
Drawing through the hand – *I hate you*.
Twirling in right hand – *I love another*.
Drawing across the right cheek – *I love you*.
Closing it – *I wish to speak to you*.
Drawing across the eye – *I am sorry*.
Letting it rest on right cheek – *Yes*.
Letting it rest on left cheek – *No*.
Open and shut – *You are cruel*.
Dropping – *We will be friends*.
Fanning slow – *I am married*.
Fanning fast – *I am engaged*.
With handle to lips – *Kiss me*.
Shut – *You have changed*.
Open wide – *Wait for me*.

Parasol Flirtation: -
Carrying it elevated in left hand – *Desiring acquaintance*.
Carrying it elevated in right hand – *You're too willing*.

Carrying closed in left hand, by side – *Follow me.*
Carrying in front of you – *No more at present.*
Carrying over shoulder – *You are too cruel.*
Closing it up – *I wish to speak with you.*
Dropping it – *I love you.*
Folding it up – *Get rid of your company.*
Letting it rest on the left cheek – *No.*
Letting it rest on the right cheek – *Yes.*
Striking on the hand – *I am much displeased.*
Swinging it to and fro by the handle on the right side – *I am married.*
Swinging same on the left side – *I am engaged.*
Tapping the chin – *I am in love with another!*
Twirling it around – *We are watched.*
Using as a fan – *Introduce me to your companion.*
With handle to lips – *Kiss me.*
Putting away – *No more at present.*

When To Marry: -

Once flirtation has led to an attachment and this has led to a courtship, the favoured outcome will be that of marriage. Whilst it seems men can marry at any age, ladies – I urge – should desist the idea of a very early marriage. Twenty-two to twenty-three years of age seems to me the most timely for an advantageous match, as a young lady will be able to understand the nature of love far better then than in her younger years. It is said that '*All those who are old enough to love deeply are old enough to marry*' and it is only with the passing of youth that deep emotions are to be understood.

It is never wise for a young woman to marry one who is younger than herself, for what protection can a boy offer against the trials and tribulations of the world? If a girl of 22 truly desires real happiness, she would do better to marry a man of 40 than a boy of 18. And in no circumstances should she be drawn into an engagement to either unless she is truly desirous of marriage. Some men will extend such offers with little true commitment for the future, so a woman must be on guard against the devious practices of a grand seducer who will promise them all, with little willingness to see through his responsibilities. Chaperones are often an able defence against such dangers.

On Choosing a Husband: -

The choice of a lifelong companion with whom you are able to build a home and raise children is not one to be made lightly. To ladies I would say: do not

'A Flirtation' by L. M.
Glackens for Puck
Magazine, c.1900,
(Library of Congress).

hurry to get married, for a hurried choice is often a bad choice, as is usually shown to be the case with a rushed decision taken in a ladies' emporium when the salesman urges you to choose a purchase. Husbands cannot be returned once you have got them home and discovered their flaws. Do not accept the first man who proposes to you, that is, unless you really love him, and it is not the first flush of youthful love, but the deep unwavering love of a devoted heart. Do not be afraid of rejecting your suitor if you know you do not love him. And above all, do NOT accept him if your only reason for doing so is because you fear you may not have another offer. It is far, far better to live and die as an old maid, than to exist as a miserable wife.

The wisest match is one where the couple have taken the time and care to see that there is a properly established and well-fitted shared character between them. Happiness in married life can come only through the understanding and harmony of both natures. I cannot counsel my young ladies more strongly: should you find yourself sought in marriage, throw aside all inherited or created affectations. As nearly as possible you must allow yourself to be seen in your '*true colours*'. Although daunting, it is a certain way to save much unhappiness for the future and will, at once and without doubt, lead to a proper and true understanding between the parties.

In choosing a husband remember there are certain immutable and unchanging points of difference between men and women from which there is no escape, as demonstrated by this simple guide:

> *When a woman becomes flurried she feels for a fan; when a man becomes flurried he feels for a cigar.*
> *Women jump at conclusions and generally hit; men reason things out logically and generally miss.*
> *A woman never sees a baby without wanting to run to it; a man never sees a baby without wanting to run from it.*
> *Women love admiration, approbation, adulation, self-immolation on the parts of others, and are often weak, vain, and frivolous. Ditto men.*
> *A woman always carries her purse in her hand, so that other women can see it; a man carries his in his inside pocket, so that his wife will not see it.*

It is known that there are just two kinds of people who should never enter into the union of marriage – firstly, '*any kind of man or woman who becomes so wedded to any special work that it absorbs their whole time and strength; if insanity is threatened to these, marriage maybe admissible, but often unadvisable*' and those who are either sadly constitutionally diseased, or those who have drunken or criminal tendencies. A final note is this: should you find the man you wish to be joined to for the rest of your days remember that a five- or ten-year courtship is a frequent but often fatal mistake. It is all very well to wait for circumstances to be prosperous, but do not let this belief in duty remove any hope of youthful companionship and early marital bliss. What better comfort can there be in times of hardship than a willing and able companion?

The Wedding Day: -
Once you have made your choice, all thoughts will turn to the wedding day. On the day of the ceremony it will be you, the bride, who is the object of supreme attention. *She is the centre to which all eyes are directed; her looks, her words and her actions, are subjects for criticism and remark.* You must be sure to act only with dignity and propriety on every occasion, as few will watch your actions without interest. Choose a gown of current fashion, with a colour to suit your complexion. The ring will be placed on the wedding finger, of which much has been both said and written. Of all that has been noted in reference to the ring, I believe the most beautiful and mystical cause is often neglected:

it is that the wedding finger is the only nerve where two principal nerves – the radial nerve and the ulnar nerve – are joined together.

A note here on the conclusion of the ceremony. It has become the usual custom of those of the middle-class rank of life to allow the bridegroom, at the end of the vows, to kiss his wife in celebration. This practice is to be decidedly avoided, as it is never done by the people of the best society. Only a bride's elderly relations are allowed to kiss her when congratulating her whilst the rest of the wedding party, friends and onlookers may pass on their best wishes. There is no finer example of the purity of such actions than the Queen herself. On the Royal wedding day, the Queen was kissed by the Duke of Sussex, but not by Prince Albert.

Once the family celebrations have been concluded and the joy of the wedding night has been realised – of which my devoted friend, Lady Petronella, will see fit to advise you – it is customary to embark upon a wedding tour. The practice is almost universal and takes place immediately after the wedding ceremony. The newly married pair might see fit to visit the Continent of Europe, or to take the waters at Bath or towards the North. It is of great necessity that these few weeks are devoted to the recreation of the newly conjoined couple, as it will allow them to find relief from the tedious anxieties, perplexities and boundaries which are imposed upon them during the practice of courtship.

In earlier times, it was customary for the bride and groom to take one or two friends along, but now they generally go alone. Should they visit the Lakes or some such fashionable place of this country, three to four weeks is considered a sufficient length of time to be away from their family. But if they are determined to visit the Continent, this cannot be done in any less than three to four months. With all this in mind I wish you the greatest success in finding a husband and securing a happy life for yourself in the future.

Women You Should Admire: -

I bring what I hope has been a helpful tome to a close with the following simple memoriam. Ours is a golden age of womanhood. Never before has society been so preoccupied with the protection of 'She, Who is Woman'. Declarations against the unjust situation of our sex have grown with rousing voracity and continue to do so as our century draws to its end. Who knows what the coming new century will bring? Will we see women in politics, taking their seats on an equal footing with men? I do not know, but one thing of which I am certain, we would not have got there without the actions, the declarations, the lives of these women:

Ada Lovelace – Poetical Scientist

The year of 1815 heralded the birth of Augusta Ada Byron, the Countess Lovelace, who bears the auspicious title of being the only legitimate daughter of Lord Byron. Although his deviant reputation has echoed throughout the corridors of our most reputable houses, it is Ada's mother, Anne Isabella Byron, Baroness Wentworth, from whom Ada received her incredible intellectual gifts. Anne was in possession of an unusually expansive and intellectually stimulating education under the tutelage of a most welcome correspondent of mine, the Cambridge radical and reformer William Frend, who had been impressed by his student's obvious aptitude and ability in the fields of mathematics and science. She had passed her remarkable gifts on to her daughter, Ada, and, when the time came, ensured that she, too, received an education in mathematics, philosophy, science and logic.

A scandal to society, my dear Baroness Wentworth separated from her terrible husband, Lord Byron, when Ada was merely a month old and Ada never saw her father again. Concerned that the 'insanity' the Baroness believed Byron suffered from would become evident in her daughter also, she pushed Ada towards the scientific fields, thus protecting her from the terrible vices that had beset her father's character.

Having excelled in the fields of mathematics, Ada soon became a favourite correspondent of Charles Babbage, the inventor of the Difference Machine and Analytical Engine. Her ability to understand logic and create mathematical theorem was magnificent, allowing her to work closely with Babbage throughout her life and contribute to the leading scientific discussions of the day, until her death in 1852. Our friends at Temple Bar remember that:

> '*Babbage was very fond of talking of Byron's daughter; to him she was always "Ada," for he had carried her in his arms as a child, and he was her friend and counsellor when she was Lady Lovelace. Kenyon had met her at Fyne Court, where she was a frequent guest, being intensely interested in Mr. Crosse's electrical experiments. Kenyon acknowledged Lady Lovelace to be a woman of remarkable intellect, but she was too mathematical for his taste. "Our family are an alternative stratification of poetry and mathematics," Lady Lovelace used to say.*'

Cora Pearl – Entrepreneur

I seek no notoriety with the inclusion of a most beloved friend. When Emma Elizabeth Crouch was born, whispered in crueller circles to have been as early as 1835, little did her family realise that she would go on to become one of Europe's most famed and renowned courtesans. Her father, Fredrick Nicholls

Illustrated Police News, 24 July 1886.

Crouch, was the composer and lyricist of that pretty little song *Kathleen Mavourneen*, but he despicably abandoned the family for America in 1849. Dearest Emma left the family home to live with her grandmother in London and it was here that she abandoned the respectable life, taking the *nom de plume* of 'Cora Pearl' and becoming the mistress of a mutual acquaintance, Mr. Robert Bignell, the proprietor of the Argyll Rooms, Windmill Street, Haymarket.

During the 1850s of my girlhood, the Argyll Rooms were renowned as a great reservoir of London West End glamour and were allowed to operate without much interference from the nosy beaks on the understanding that the goings on of these rooms would dam up for the evening all the brightest and most brilliant in one place, to stop it from overflowing into the Haymarket, Regent and other streets, until most decent folks were at home.

After some time spent with Bignell, Cora travelled to Paris, where she was rumoured to have been accompanied by Robert who posed as her husband.

Here, she fell in love with the city, as I did upon visiting her there, and decided to set herself up in her preferred trade, that of a courtesan. At the height of her hard-won fame, her list of lovers counted royalty and celebrity and I received a letter from her to say that she was known as *'the scandal and the toast of Paris'*. This notorious demimondaine of the French Empire accumulated staggeringly vast riches from the wealthy persons who sustained the Empire and had no shame in the public nature of her profession, refusing to be shamed into conducting her affairs in private. Most of us were not so brave.

In 1864, I remember witnessing a gentleman attempting to persuade her to live a more virtuous life, and remonstrated with her that she was breaking the hearts of many of the young men in Paris. Cora replied, *'How am I to provide the luxuries you see around you, by any other means than those I now employ? And believe me, no young man is duped who does not choose to be so.'* I was, at this time, staying in the small hotel she owned – most exquisitely furnished – which was often the base of her operations in Paris. It was here that envoys of the Emperor would often attempt to secure the return of the money some young foolish nobleman had squandered on her; in one instant they appeared at the request of the nobleman's mother. Cora sent them away empty handed, retorting, *'I do but follow the trade I have chosen.'*

I will always be saddened by her end, one whom the newspapers had scrambled over in their haste to include her clothes, hair, and adventures in their pages. Although able to enjoy a public yet scandalous career for much of her life, Cora's final affair was the one that would be her ultimate undoing. She began a most ill-advised relationship with Alexandre Duval, the son of the butcher, whose father had founded a chain of very cheap restaurants. For the two years that followed his father's death, Duval pursued Cora relentlessly, spending on her, and her stables and lap dogs, his entire fortune of 17 million francs. When the money finally ran out Cora refused to see him and Duval was devastated. One day, he managed to force his way into her presence and discharged a pistol at his temples intending to blow his brains out right at her feet, but his hand slipped, leaving his face badly wounded.

The entire affair was reported in the press, including the papers in London, as was Cora's reaction to his display. As Duval lay at her feet, her tears were not for the wounded boy, but instead for the new carpet on which he was bleeding. The knowledge of this apparent lack of feeling led to Cora's ultimate removal from society and she retired to pen her memoirs, dying in 1886 before I could reach her. She remained defiant until the end, writing, *'I have never deceived anyone, for I have never belonged to anyone. My independence was all my wealth: I have known no other happiness.'*

60

Josephine Butler – Women's Advocate

Few women in our great century have fought so hard or struggled so long in the name of 'Womankind' as Josephine Butler. From her birth in 1828 to her death in 1906, Mrs. Butler dedicated her every waking moment to the cause of protecting women from those parts of society that would demean and betray them. She did not see fallen women as the great curse that so many of our writers and reporters would have you believe, but rather that they were the victims of man's vice, a social understanding weighted far too heavily in favour of men. Her investigative journalism, long before the work of W.T. Stead, exposed the terrible realities of the Contagious Diseases Act, and her determination to see them repealed brought her international acclaim. She deserved the title of one of *'the grandest heroines of our time'*.

Devoting herself to the moral work from which many sensitive women have seen to shrink by blaming their natural delicacy, Mrs. Butler alone was possessed of a most stern sense of duty. It was her unfailing and overwhelming sympathy with the wronged and suffering amongst women which saw her continually brave public opinion. She endured with great calmness the scoffs and accusations of vulgar men for the sake of the fallen of her sex. Without her work, their position in life would have suffered all the more from the men and women who sought to exploit them.

Annie Besant – Political Reformer

In 1888, the Bryant and May Match Factory in Bow, London witnessed a revolution. The women and girls of the factory had suffered terrible working conditions – 14-hour days, horrible diseases and little relief in their pay, to name but a few. The captivating Annie Besant had recently reported on the conditions in *The Link*, a weekly paper, and in retaliation, the owners had ordered their workers to sign a document stating that the report contained only falsehoods. They refused and one worker was dismissed, a most despicable tactic designed to scare the rest of the women into obedience. They refused to be cowed and soon all the women walked out. As the strike raged on, a deputation of 100 women marched to the offices of *The Link*, hoping that Annie would be able to assist them in furthering their cause.

She did so, speaking at meetings and engaging the help of her long time collaborator, the MP Charles Bradlaugh, who spoke of the women's working conditions in parliament. The firm bowed under political pressure and improved both the working conditions and pay for its employees. But this was not the first time Annie had joined her voice to the cause of working women. Born in 1847, she had married a vicar at the age of 20, to quickly bearing him

Illustrated Police News, 21 July 1888.

two children. Here, Annie's life could have quickly passed into that of wife and mother, but it was not to be. She was a radical and a free thinker, whose political and religious leanings were in total opposition to those of her husband, and after six years of marriage, she left him.

Moving to London, Annie found friends in the radical circles and soon became a well-known speaker and writer on many issues concerning the rights of the individual. Her notoriety was assured in 1877 when she was prosecuted alongside Charles Bradlaugh under the Obscene Publications Act of 1857 for printing and distributing a pamphlet, originally published by Dr. Charles Knowlton in 1832, to the working men and women of London. This pamphlet – *Fruits of Philosophy*, a copy of which I keep by my bedside – was seen as dangerous as its contents set out clearly the advocacy of methods for limiting reproduction, whilst still enjoying the act of physical love. Annie was unrepentant. She argued that the limitation of the family would destroy pauperism and that all she herself and Mr. Bradlaugh had ever taught was the belief that the loyal and faithful love between one man and one woman was the highest ideal of human love.

Queen Victoria – Regina

Who is a more fitting epitaph of our age, and of womanhood, than her most Glorious Majesty, Alexandrina Victoria, Queen of the Kingdom of Great Britain and Ireland and Empress of India? What words could I utter that would convey the life of the wife and mother who has been the figurehead of such an age as this? Her devotion to her family, her husband and her country are examples for us all, but it is her devotion to love that is the most important. I can think of no better voice than her own for this, from the morning after her wedding. I can but hope it is as all young brides will feel.

Queen Victoria, by J.E Mayall, c.1862, (Library of Congress).

I never, never spent such an evening!! My dearest dearest dear Albert sat on a footstool by my side, and his excessive love and affection gave me feelings of heavenly love and happiness, I never could have hoped to have felt before! He clasped me in his arms, and we kissed each other again and again! His beauty, his sweetness and gentleness, - really how can I ever be thankful enough to have such a Husband! - At ½ p.10 I went and undressed and was very sick, and at 20 m. p.10 we both went to bed; (of course in one bed), to lie by his side, and in his arms, and on his dear bosom, and be called by names of tenderness, I have never yet heard used to me before - was bliss beyond belief! Oh! This was the happiest day of my life! - May God help me to do my duty as I ought and be worthy of such blessings!

Volume 3

The Rev. J. J. James's Advice for the Single Man

On Manliness – Flirtation – Contraception –
How to Choose a Wife by the Shape of her Legs – The Age to Marry –
The Wedding Day

We, all of us, have a calling in life and for the young man, fresh from his youth and schoolboy activities, the modern world holds much in the way of excitements and abounds in curious experiences. My own feelings run to the knowledge that, without proper guidance, the moral fortitude of man can become somewhat questionable; and without instruction, a gentleman can find himself quickly beset by troubles on all sides. It is my intention to impart a modicum of advice to those who have yet to find happiness within the marital union, as well as to offer a guiding hand in how this may be most quickly achieved.

I speak also to those men of the world who engage in activities both immoral and dangerous to their sex. Do not think I am unwise to your adventures and do not think to dismiss the advice held within the pages of this volume, for it may well prevent further catastrophe from befalling you.

On Manliness: -

I shall begin with a declaration of what a man truly is: he is one who is, at all times, courageous in danger, meeting the trials of his daily life (should they come) with a bravery and nobility especially found in the male sex. He boldly faces misfortune and in every way you will find him to act the part of a truthful and upright man. A woman looks to find in a man all that she believes to be manly and these qualities will inspire in her the feelings of love. On no account should a man act in opposition to his character in the game of love, for what can be more absurd than to see a man woo a girl under the pretence that he is different from what he really is? It is a most disingenuous act, one that will only end in unhappiness and ruin for both parties.

c. 1883, (Library of Congress).

There is occasion for some men to believe that love, and all its trappings, is only found through a slavish deference to the wishes of their lady love. This is a ridiculous idea and will only lead to boredom for all concerned. A respectful manner is the most appropriate, rather than mawkish fawning, which no woman of good sense should ever allow. Always seek to make your conduct towards her show you to be straightforward, studiously respectful and manly. I must strongly advise you to always speak to women as if they were rational beings and not the mere playthings of an hour.

Should your overtures of love be met with a welcoming reaction, remember that you should not be too forward in boasting of your previous conquests, as no woman will welcome such conversation. Worse still would be to refer to those ephemeral beings you have loved in the past. Such conduct will only ever be seen to be in the worst possible taste. It is also very liable to breed angry and jealous feelings within the listener, feelings which are easily roused and far more difficult to quell than the speaker would expect. Whilst jealousy can, at times, be an added inflammation to the passions, an unduly jealous lover exposes himself as an unattractive husband – something you would be wise not

Eugen Sandow by Napoleon Sarony, c.1893,(Library of Congress).

Eugen Sandow by George Steckel, c.1894, (Library of Congress).

to do. I would also argue that the same rules could be applied to a lady, as her conduct should be examined as much as your own.

I can but recommend you follow the example of that most masculine of men – the 'Monarch of Muscle'– Eugen Sandow. Although born in Prussia in 1867 under the name of Fredrich Wilhelm Muller, Sandow has rapidly become a moniker that has spread across the globe. When he first appeared at the London Aquarium in 1889 his breathtaking abilities in the field of physical excellence entranced many. Although he is defined as a 'strong man', it is his willingness to teach a system of physical education that warrants my recommendation. In his 'Institutes of Physical Culture', Sandow advises the best methods that will take a man from a puny delicate youth to a prodigiously muscular being such as Sandow himself. His inestimable strength allows him to tear three packs of cards – when placed all together – directly down the middle and to lift a 300lb barbell. It is quite a sight to behold.

For those inspired by the great Sandow's physical perfection, may I recommend an investment in his greatest machine, '*Sandow's Own Combined Developer*' as used daily by pianists, singers, painters, actors, doctors, cyclists of both sexes, and those whose health is in decline. There is no exercise so pleasant or invigorating and it can be purchased from F. A. Lumley's Athletic Stores, 127 Leith Street, Edinburgh, for no more than 12s 6d.

Flirtation: -

The modern world is full of entrancing members of the opposite sex, for whom a young man is seen as an object of the greatest interest. A gentleman should be aware that this might not always be a reflection on his character, but rather on his marital worth. Those who have acquired property, or have found themselves to have been left some, can flirt violently and with unlimited privileges. He can marry at 25, 30, 40 or 50. It is his money that renders him a superior being and a most eligible match in the eyes of prospective mother-in-law. It is often unfortunate that this becomes his own belief, too. Those with property are often able to enjoy lengthy courting days and they find themselves indulging in many lovers who would not, perhaps, be so enamoured with their company should money be unimportant. Beware the risks of

Unknown Man, Seely's Art Gallery, c.1860-69, (Library of Congress).

illicit connections with individuals who seek their own personal betterment through an attachment to you.

If you have taken heed of my warnings, then the risk of attaching yourself to an undesirable person will be greatly lessened. I do not subscribe to the notion that a young man in the modern world will not act on his natural urges and whilst their proper home exists within the marital union, I feel it is timely to offer advice for those who seek to gain experience in these matters.

To successfully form a connection to a woman whom you admire, you must be adequately versed in the art of flirtation. Flirtation is a skill both men and women subscribe to and without it very little would be achieved other than a deep and contented friendship. Flirtation does not necessarily involve the bestowing of gifts or letters; it is, in its most intimate form, the secret language used by a courting couple to discuss their intention. What follows is a detailed understanding of that language with a guide for use and interpretation.

Flirtation by the Eye: -
Winking the right eye – *I love you.*
Winking the left eye – *I hate you.*
Winking both eyes – *Yes.*
Winking both eyes at once – *We are watched.*
Winking right eye twice – *I am engaged.*
Winking left eye twice – *I am married.*
Dropping the eyelids – *May I kiss you?*
Raising the eyebrows – *Kiss me.*
Closing the right eye slowly – *Try and love me.*
Closing the left eye slowly – *You are beautiful.*
Placing the right forefinger to right eye – *Do you love me?*
Placing right forefinger to left eye – *You are handsome.*
Placing right little finger to right eye – *Aren't you ashamed?*

Flirtation by Glove: -
Holding with tips downwards – *I wish to be acquainted.*
Twirling around the fingers – *Be careful! We are watched.*
Right hand with the naked thumb exposed – *Kiss me.*
Left hand with the naked thumb exposed – *Do you love me?*
Using them as fan – *Introduce me to your company.*
Smoothing them out gently – *I wish I were with you.*
Holding them loose in the left hand – *Be contented.*

Biting the tips – *I wish to be rid of you very soon.*
Folding up carefully – *Get rid of your company.*
Striking over the hand – *I am displeased.*
Drawing halfway on left hand – *Indifference.*
Clenching them (rolled up) in right hand – *No.*
Dropping one of them – *Yes.*
Striking them over shoulder – *Follow me.*
Ends of tips to lips – *Do you love me?*
Tossing them up gently – *I am engaged.*
Turning them inside out – *I hate you.*
Dropping both of them – *I love you.*
Tapping the chin – *I love another.*
Putting them away – *I am vexed.*

Flirtation using a Hat: -

Carrying it in the right hand – *Desirous of an acquaintance.*
Carrying it in the left hand – *I hate you.*
Running the finger around the crown – *I love you.*
Running the hand around the rim – *I hate you.*
To wear on the right side of the head – *No.*
To wear on the left side of the head – *Yes.*
To wear on the back of the head – *I wish to speak with you.*
To incline towards the nose – *We are watched.*
Putting it behind you – *I am married.*
Putting it in front of you – *I am single.*
Carrying in the hand by the crown – *Follow me.*
Putting it under the right arm – *Wait for me.*
Putting it under the left arm – *I will be at the gate at 8 p.m.*
Putting the hat on the head straight – *All for the present.*

Contraception: -

Whilst many scholars would submit that it is virtually impossible for public women to find themselves with child after a connection, due to the degradation of their genital organs, it has been my experience that this may not be true in all cases. To make sure you keep the line of your generation free of pollutants, or should your seduction involve a respectable lady and you desire to protect her reputation – gentlemanly behaviour is important even then – I offer the following practical advice for the art of checking conception.

HYDE PARK LOVERS.

Illustrated Police News, 30 November 1895

1. A woman is most likely to conceive if she engages in copulation directly after a menstrual turn, or as they are often referred to, 'the monthlies'.

2. It is clear that nothing short of entire withdrawal can be depended upon.

3. Use of the Baudruche, or condom: this device is a covering used by the man and consists of a very delicate animal skin placed over his genital organs and held in place by a ribbon. It has been used with great effect to secure from syphilitic infections. It is by no means calculated to come into general use. However, should you feel it a worthwhile endeavour, instructions for creation and maintenance are included in later volumes.

4. Another useful invention requires its implementation prior to the act of copulation. The woman places inside her vagina a very delicate piece

of sponge that has been moistened with water. Immediately after the event it should be withdrawn by a very narrow ribbon, which has been attached to the sponge previous to the connection. I would advise the reader that this check has yet to prove to be a true preventative.

5. The use of a female syringe, which may be found at the shop of every apothecary for a shilling or less, is another most important check. It consists of syringing the vagina with a solution of sulphate of zinc, of alum, pearlash, or any salt that acts chemically on the semen. Most important a consideration is that the solution produces no unfavourable effect on the woman who uses it. I have been led to believe that in all probability a vegetable astringent would be of equal effect. It has been suggested that an infusion of white oak bark, or of red rose leaves, or of nut galls and the like, are an admirable base for the connection. To this, a lump of the aforementioned salts, which must be equal to the size of a chestnut, must then be dissolved in a pint of water. Make the solution weaker or stronger to protect against any irritation of the parts to which it is applied. This action must be taken immediately after the connection has ceased in its actions. I am aware that the use of this check above all others will require the woman to leave her bed for a few moments, but in this I see its only objection. A word in its favour, it should be said, is that it costs nearly nothing; it is a guaranteed check against conception; it is the office of the female to carry out, and not the office of the man; it is to be used after, rather than prior to the act of connection; and last, but by no means least, it is most conducive to female cleanliness and preserves her genital organs from relaxation and many forms of disease.

How to Choose a Wife by the Shape of Her Legs: -

The great French poet Pierre Jules Theophile Gautier (1811–1872) once proclaimed, '*Show me the leg, and I will read the mind.*' Leading on from this – and remembering from earlier volumes all you have learnt from the practice of reading your beloved's character in their physical attributes – I feel it is most pertinent to present you with a handy reference guide for the easiest way to choose your future intended: by the shape of her legs.

It may be that you were unaware of such possibilities and, make no mistake, it will take all of your most gentlemanly attributes to observe the lower legs unseen – for such observations will be considered greatly improper in respectable company. But I am sure, once you are well versed in this understanding, you will indeed choose a proper and well-domesticated wife.

Artist: Steven Kirk.

1. No woman on the stage will make a respectable wife. Although most easily observed, she has shown every part of herself to a paying audience. *Distrust Stage Legs.*

2. Sturdy legs, with a neat ankle and sensible shoes will be best for a man who desires an intellectual companion. *Clever, but not a Blue Stocking.*

3. Heavy legs and flat shoes are signifiers of a most coarse nature. *Avoid this as you would the Pox.*

4. A delicately turned ankle, feminine boots and stocking on a gently curving leg. *You may surely go for this girl.*

5. If you constantly observe the backs of your beloved's legs during your courtship, remember this: *You will have to play second fiddle.*

6. Thin, yet muscular legs are best for a man who likes his household run with military precision. *Will get up early in the morning and blow up the servants.*

7. There is one accompaniment to the delicately turned ankle, which many a man will find a great source of happiness. *A combination of Red Hair and Ankles like these – Propose At Once!!*

8. The legs of a masculine woman. *Fly from a woman so endowed – she will be literally no use at all!*

The Age To Marry: -

To protect from the sin of *onanism* and after the youthful forays into the world of industry and honour, a gentleman's thoughts should turn to that of marriage. I would say that there should be no hurry to enter into the marital union and public opinion would agree that no man should seriously consider marriage until he has achieved the age of at least 25. Before this age he should not be considered manly or have been educated enough in worldly matters to successfully maintain the trials and bonds that marriage will place upon him.

I think it pertinent to also say that there are many types of persons who should not attempt to marry at any age. Any match they attempt to make is certain to be a failure, especially in the matrimonial sense. They are often the best of society; they may compose great operas, paint great pictures, acquire the greatest fortunes or write books of great worth, but it is to these, and these alone, which they should be wedded. When a man turns his mind away from the life of a bachelor and to the wedded bliss of the marital union, in choosing an advantageous match there are three rules that he must rigidly observe:

1. You must be sure to choose a woman worthy of your respect, as well as your love and devotion.

2. Be most careful to choose a companionable woman, for she will be your partner for life; your fireside conversation; your old age comforter; and with her you will spend the dawn and dusk of your coming years.

3. Make quite sure she has been *domesticated.*

Once you have made your choice of future mate, be advised that a protracted courtship will never commonly be a woman's wish. In the cases when they have been known to occur they are commonly an injustice to her, so it is likely that she will only submit to such a fate under protest. This may take the form of a silent protest, one which is all the more dangerous to the future happiness of the intended as it causes a residual of poor feeling and unhappiness to build up in the submissive party before the marriage has even begun.

Annie Revere for Edelweiss Brew, c.1898, (Library of Congress).

Another inadvisable action is that of an old man marrying a much younger bride. It is somewhat common, but I would say, highly unsafe. This union, which can only be described as the action of one developing into womanhood being conjoined for her most favourable years to one who is only declining into manhood, is akin to '*putting new wine into old bottles*'. I can state it no more clearly than this: any man past his prime should never consider marriage to a much younger woman. He will, in all honesty, find it more convenient to hire a nurse.

The Wedding Day: -
Once a successful courtship has been pursued and you have made a suitable

selection for your wife, and, most importantly, she has given her consent, the arrival of the wedding day brings certain duties that befall the bridegroom alone to carry out. Custom must be followed with regards to the traditions and demands of this most important of days, beginning with the presentation of the bride's bouquet. The groom must furnish each bridesmaid as well as the bride herself, with a gift and bouquet. He is to make sure the house has been adequately furnished in every detail to please his bride, except with regard to the house and table linen, which is the reserve of the bride and her family.

'Cupid's Candidate' by F. Burr Opper, for Puck Magazine, c.1896, (Library of Congress).

The wedding ring, the singular and most symbolic moment of the wedding day, must also be provided by the bridegroom. He must also provide the carriage that shall escort both himself and his best man to the church at the correct time. It is the duty of the bridegroom to pay the fees to the clergyman and the clerk, which will ensure the legality of the marriage.

Once all of these duties have been carried out, he will wait, accompanied by the best man, at the altar until the bride arrives. She will then take her place on his left hand side. At the right and proper moment, when asked, he will produce the ring that will become, to all who see it, a symbol of their union.

A word on the costume and usual dress of the bridegroom on his wedding day: it has been advised by those in the highest echelons of society that the clothing for this most important of days should consist of *'a very dark blue frock-coat, light coloured trousers, a light or white scarf or tie, patent boots, and a new hat'*.

And here ends the guidance I wish to impart to both young boy and gentleman. Seek always to be the best of men and you shall have every success in life, love and industry.

Lady Petronella Von-Hathsburg's Guide to Marital Relations

*Some Thoughts on Marriage – The Roles of Husband and Wife –
A Woman's Inferiority – Wedded Bliss – The Wedding Night –
The Art of Conception – Sterility – Inadvisable Sexual Congress –
The Importance of Pleasure – Pregnancy – Family Life – Divorce*

Dear Reader, one of the most important events occurring in human life is that of marriage. Indeed, where it is known that True Love exists there will always be found a happy home. This is one in which – we would fearlessly assert – lives the ultimate union of love, truth and faithfulness. These harmonious elements, shared only between a man and a wife, lead to a state of wedded bliss which is thus proclaimed to be the nearest to human happiness that it is permitted for mortals to enjoy on this earth.

Within this sacred bond lies the opportunity for generation: an act of union between the physical bodies that is encouraged by society and which results in the continuation of the human species. The purpose of this volume is to act as guide, confidante and authority on the roles married life assigns to us: to promote its harmony; to delicately define its purpose; and to aid in its success.

Although we are often told of much unhappiness that has been found in wedded life, it seems that this has often been caused by the thoughtlessness of those who have joined their lots together for reasons that do not reflect either the sanctity or seriousness of the bond they have undertaken. The advice given to you in the preceding volumes plainly states that the correct reason for marriage is True Love and advises against any foolhardy unions resulting from a lack of maturity, or for want of True Love, which in all cases – it must be continually asserted – should accompany the marriage vows.

Having attained the marriageable state, and after the conflicting emotions of the wedding day, there must come the wedding night. We think it advisable to present a few delicate hints to the young and to those who are anxiously looking forward to the first consummation of the connubial vow. The advice contained within these pages will not only aid the passing of daily life, but also allows us to discuss the most natural and sacred act itself. Furthermore, we set out the means by which we may not only increase the pleasures of the act, but also equally add to the comfort and happiness of our mates and ensure an offspring that is both healthy and vigorous.

Some Thoughts on Marriage: -
To avoid a unsatisfactory union, the mode of courting in England has given those 'courting couples' a more than excellent opportunity for character study. Modern methods of **Physiology**, **Physiognomy**, or **Phrenology** have all aided in deepening an understanding of the character of a person's intended. Yet in the years before these methods were discovered, men and women understood each other through general experience, analysis and keen observation. Methods you may use to unlock the secrets of your beloved are many, yet it is important to note that whilst some people's character can be known in five minutes, others require studying for many months. All the charts and fortune-telling alone will not allow you to come to a more adequate conclusion that could not have been reached by a timely observance of the power of conversation. For the success of a marital union relies heavily on the husband and wife having a good knowledge and understanding of each other's character. Without such an understanding, the union will fail.

Above all things, True Love is of the utmost importance not only for the happiness of the two persons involved, but for the success of their future offspring. Any union where there is a want of love between man and wife will cause barrenness, sterility, or far worse, the propagation of an ill-looking, sour and spiritless offspring. Let this be a warning to the Reader whom we encourage to take most virulent heed of this elemental knowledge. For as it is said, '*If their hearts are not united in love, how should their seed unite to bring forth a comely offspring, if any at all?*'

The Roles of Husband and Wife: -

To begin, let us approach the marital roles of the husband and wife. Sadly, it is important to remember that the art of getting a husband is far easier than the art of keeping him. Men find more freedom in public life than women, and for a wife, the strength of her bond to children, home and furniture will far outweigh the difficulties faced by a truant husband who has gone to the Antipodes or to the dogs. She, the more beholden of the two, is less likely to depart from those responsibilities.

It is important to understand that whilst the lure of public life is often exerted over men, it is the wife who creates the shelter needed when they wish to retreat from it. Her importance to his happiness is paramount and whilst any noodle-headed husband may be gratified by the idea that this means she is his *possession*, he would be advised to dismiss such ridiculous notions immediately from his mind. The husband provides the domestic hearth and

c. 1902, (Library of Congress).

home. It is his duty to render it as agreeable and cheerful as possible within the financial restraints placed upon him. However, once provided, it becomes the domain of his wife. He is not to interfere unnecessarily in household affairs, as this is an intrusion into a department that does not belong to him. Home and hearth are her domain.

It has been suggested that a sensible wife will never attempt to dispute the authority of her husband. We would not disagree, as long as the husband is a fair and just man whose influence on the family home is one of tender understanding. A wife's duty is to be a stalwart companion to her husband, mother to their children, and to run the home as an example of shining domesticity to all who cross its threshold. But only half the duty rests on women. Indeed the other half is the clear responsibility of men. To this we say: What about husbands? Where does their duty lie?

A husband's main duty is to work hard and ensure the financial security which provides the home. All other domestic duties are the care of his wife. But, if he cannot provide these, or, by worsening character, will not provide them, then he can blame no one but himself. It should be noted that an unfortunate change in circumstance can often influence a man's ability to provide for his wife and family. In this respect, we urge all our readers to know that it is wise for a man to consult his wife in any case where trouble should assail him. Husbands should not despise the counsel that is suggested by a loving and tender wife. Often have men found themselves to be extricated from the direst troubles by following the advice of a clever, caring and thoughtful woman.

A Woman's Inferiority: -

It has sometimes been the case that a prideful and careless husband might dismiss the counsel of his wife. We would assert that this is to do with his misunderstanding of the notion of property, whereby those with property are viewed as greater authorities than those without. For all who study our system with regard to property, there must be agreement that young women are generally dealt a hard hand, as the transference of property is often settled upon the male line. The peculiarly English mania for founding a family and perpetuating a line relies on the dominance in property of its male offspring. This exists as an outmoded and old-fashioned system that seeks to enrich one child and beggar the rest. Most commonly, the eldest son is left the lion's share and any other sons are sought a profession. As for the daughters, a fashionable education is all that is available, unless they take advantage of their feminine traits and attempt to secure the richest husband that can be found. It is an unmitigated wrong to endow the sons with property to the exclusion of the daughters. This system propagates the savage old idea of female inferiority and weakness, and a reverence for such time-honoured absurdities is somehow maintained in our modern world.

What would the world be if every son was made an equal heir, or every daughter an equal heiress with the sons? Why not? Why should we view it as an accident to be born a girl? It should be no disqualification in obtaining simple status. How differently the marriageable state would seem if both parties brought equal weight to their union. Banished to the darkness would be that oft-expressed desire one hears so frequently in social circles, '*I Wish I Had Been Born A Man*'. No man has ever lamented that he is not a woman.

This dependence, this sense of inferiority on the part of young Englishwomen leads them to develop impractical habits that are only a result of their wrong positioning. This degrading dependence has only one outcome: it renders the marriage state as a necessity to women, but not to men. For the man has his property and the freedom it grants him, for his whole life, whilst the woman sees property as either her father's or her brother's or her husband's. The sole injustice of not dowering daughters equally with sons must always be borne in mind when a husband speaks with his wife, which at all times should be done with the utmost regard. This inequality has lead to an innumerable amount of unsuitable matches and worse, for those without any substantial marriage portion at all are left to add to an ever-increasing catalogue of old maids.

Wedded Bliss: -

Having taken into account the foundations of a union, let us now explore how best to maintain matrimonial harmony. In this regard, we speak solely to the husband, as from him all examples of behaviour and good manners must be taken. In all things, he must be seen to be master of the house. He must act towards his wife with a strict integrity at all times. He must never be found to have broken his word to her on any occasion. This is an unforgivable offence.

After marriage, he must always show that his love and affection towards her has suffered no abatement, treating her in a most becoming manner to reassure her that he has the same strength of feeling towards her as he did before the courtship ended. At all times, he should treat her with the utmost kindness, making her aware that she is both his friend and confidante for all occasions, and, as we have already suggested, he should consult her when he is faced with any perplexing difficulties. Above all others, it is his wife that carries an anxious and continual concern for her husband's welfare. Although the laws of this land grant a husband power over his wife, it must only ever be used in a paternal

Illustrated Police News, 5 March 1898.

and friendly manner; never must it be allowed to become either despotic or magisterial. A tyrannical husband is no husband at all. From birth we are taught that woman was placed on earth to be *with* man, as his companion, not that she was given *to* him, as his possession.

The union of marriage is the combination of singular elements, each with their unique ideas of the world. Whilst greater authorities have spoken fully on the matter of property and on the marriage state, it must always be remembered that '*a woman betrothed to a man bears all her portion, and with a mighty love pats it into the hands of her husband, and says; I have nothing of my own:- my goods, my portion, my body, and my mind are yours*'. It is the duty of a man to care for all she brings on her wedding day and all that comes after it. Yet – it is important to note – a man who will give way to every petty whim of his lady love or his wife is a most unfortunate animal whom many people will rightly be likely to despise.

The Wedding Night: -

Having discussed the myriad of ways in which husbands and wives should learn to understand one another, let us now turn our thoughts to the sole purpose of marriage: the ultimate act of human nature, that of generation which begins with the wedding night and continues throughout married life. It is an essential part of marital relations, without which much disharmony to the relationship has been known to creep in. The institution of marriage exists for the sole purpose of preventing any illicit connections occurring between the sexes, and the wedding night is one that has been often longed for by both parties. In general, those devotions to Hymen's shire will be beset with pleasure, hopes and joys, as many men are of such gentle and loving natures towards their new

*'Late for breakfast',
c.1901, (Library of
Congress).*

wives that they will most diligently seek out any advice regarding this matter that shall be of benefit to both parties. For such men this volume is indeed intended; it is also designed for the benefit of women so to guide and initiate those for whom the act of generation is an unknown experience.

As already suggested vis-à-vis the understanding of each other's characters, the natural state of reproduction requires a state of utter and complete frankness that must be observed between the married pair. There must be no private reserves on the wedding night and each one must allow their soul to be as open as their arms. They must aspire to find a shared mutual freedom running through their general conversation; unfeigned and open innocence are the most necessary accomplishments to a successful endeavour. The virgin state of ignorance is often attended by a private coyness or faintness, but now, in the bold light of enjoyment and knowledge this must be utterly abolished. The wedded night delight forms part of the matrimonial state to which access should never be denied and the unlocking of the virginal cabinet become a source of untold pleasure for the years ahead of them.

Perhaps it would be better to speak plainly. When a woman goes to bed with a man, or a man goes to bed with a woman, any foolish coldness, or peevish argument must be left off with their modesty – in their clothes. Some are taught that feigned disinterest or displeasure is a respectable trait. It is not. This is a wedlock fault and must not be encouraged.

One must remember that the institution of marriage has been eternally linked to the act of generation. Only within the marital union can the security be found which will benefit both the husband and wife and why a fulfilment of the most natural urges must wait until after the bonds of marriage have been unified. It is our deepest regret to inform the Reader that certain beguiling and vicious blaggards will attempt to seduce an innocent young woman into a physical union with false offers of marriage. What sorrow, what bitterness can result from affairs such as these? What wretchedness is heaped upon the poor offspring of such a union, begot only in falsehood and insincerity. Left to nurse in silence and shame, the woman is left damaged and rendered untouchable by respectable society. Scarce has the torch of hymen been lit than it is then extinguished, or worse, left to the streets and the enumerable sorrows which nightly roam them.

The Art of Conception: -
Once the joys of the wedding night have passed and the physical pleasures have been explored, the wedded couple's mind will turn to the successful act of generation. We shall now recommend the wisdom of certain authorities as to

how this can be most practically achieved. As with all things, the circumstances in which the young couple find themselves have the most direct implications upon the accomplishment of this endeavour. Indeed, amongst physiologists there has been strident debate arising from speculations as to what effect can be found in the climate and season, as well as the effect of temperament and age of both the husband and wife upon the reproductive power of human beings. It has been suggested that a more temperate and warm climate will be found to be far more beneficial in exciting the copulative desires, whilst those who find themselves located in the more uncongenial and frigid situations of the northern or more remote parts of the earth will struggle to equal the reproductive success of their more southern counterparts. This, perhaps, should be noted when planning one's wedding tour.

Let us now discuss the act itself. As within the marriage union, the roles of man and woman in the physical union are also clearly set out before us. The most important part performed by the husband in the successful act – resulting in a reproduction of his line and a continuation of the species – consists of a sole purpose: to elicit the orgasm of his wife and deposit his semen into her vagina. The importance of the female orgasm is this: without it, her seed will not be released and no child will be formed in her womb. During the connection, the woman shall be able to perceive that her release of seed is near. This will arrive as a '*tinkling pleasure*' within her body, which she must advertise to her husband immediately. This is so that at the very same instant, in a shared moment, he too may also give forth his seed. By this collision, by that very meeting of seeds, the conception shall be made and will result in a child being formed and ultimately born. And so to make certain the success of this act, after both have spent, it is of the utmost importance that on no account does the husband extricate himself from his wife's embrace. If he does so, the air may strike into the open womb. This will corrupt the seeds within and destroy any hope of their success before they have been perfectly mixed together. Once the man has later departed, perhaps to retire to his own rooms, we would urge the woman to lie still and to do so most quietly. She must lay her legs or thighs across one another. Most importantly, she must be sure to raise them up a little, by aid of a pillow or other such device. This will make certain that no motion or downward situation will allow for the seed to be shed or spilt. During this time, and without exception, she must not talk, or sneeze, or cough, and especially not nag or chide her husband, but instead give herself utterly to both rest and quietness until a suitable surfeit of time has passed.

Women, we have found, are most likely to conceive a day or two after their monthly bleed has ended. However, we do not suggest that this allows for the instant resumption of marital concourse. In the act of love, time and place must be understood to be of the utmost importance, as any element of fear or surprise on the part of the woman will hinder future conception. There are other practical elements that will work against a successful connection. Women are far less likely to conceive during the week before their monthly bleed and so this must be taken into account during the timing of the act itself. Emotional discontent is yet another wonderful hinderer to conception, for both husband and wife. Each must seek to find a contented mind, or else they risk the vital heat needed for a successful physical connection being diverted from the bodily circumference, to its centre; this will only serve to dry out, consume and waste the body and spirit of the dejected party.

Sterility: -

Previous volumes of this work have discussed the checking of intercourse in illicit connections to make sure that children are not brought into the world that cannot be cared for. Whilst we would also promote the use of such methods within the marital union should the creation of offspring be untimely, for those who wish to improve their ability to conceive we offer this instruction. The most beneficial aid to removing the most common cases of sterility can be found by exercising in the open air; a healthy diet of nourishing food; and the hygienic comfort of flannel dress. Those who seek a cure from their sterility would do well to follow all we have advised and understand that these methods are to be observed by both husband and wife. For persons who seek a tonic to aid in the reproductive state, our most highly regarded method – one, which we believe, treats both princess and pauper with equal success – is as follows:

Procure from the local blacksmith some scales which have fallen from his anvil; or some steel filings, small and numerous. Place these into old cider, or if you prefer, wine – although it must be noted cider has the most success. After they have steeped in a jar for a week or so, take between two and three times a day, as long as it can be borne without disturbing the patient's stomach.

Inadvisable Sexual Congress: -

Whilst the success of connection is reliant on many factors, we think it important to suggest moments where the physical union is certainly not advisable. It is true that there are times when sexual connection *must* be avoided, under any circumstances, although this may be a disappointing lesson for some to learn. Immediately after a hearty meal is the most dangerous time to attempt the act of generation as it results in the stomach becoming distended with meats or in the system being highly exhilarated by the potent effects of wine. Any form of sexual commerce must be avoided in these circumstances, as we are reliably informed of cases of apoplexy having been induced by the understandable excitement of a connection. The risks of this are certain death, most understandably distressing for all involved.

It is also important that if the couple wish for the production of a fair offspring, they understand that the work of generation must not be faintly or drowsily performed. This is one of the most notorious causes that make wise men beget foolish children; and we can plainly see evident in our society the result of such connections are a race so far short of their parents' nature, manners and generosity, that some will wonder how they could have come to be. It is clear that the efforts that begot them were wanting of the true spirit of love to animate the conception.

But from where does this fault spring? And who is to blame? There are two distinct causes known to us: either the father's intolerable indifference in observing the *rites of love,* a very capital sin and one which we feel is most capably remedied by careful attention to this work or the fault that proceeds from too passionate a devotion to physical love. This, indeed, is a fault of the far more innocent side. The difference between the two is this: any husband who dismisses the importance of his observance of the *rites of love* for a woman's pleasure is seen to be committing no less than a certain violation of his marriage vows, whilst a shared committed zeal to the act of union can result in the over toiling of the entire generative faculty, often the result of a young couple's passion for the newly inhabited marital bed. It is the responsibility of the husband that, to aid the success of a connection, he does not allow himself to become overstimulated and thus tire himself out. We must insist on taking one's time and pleasure in the act to ensure reproductive success. Once a connection has borne fruit, he is free to tumble with his wife as fast and as headlong as he sees fit, but until that moment, care must be taken by both to make sure they remain fit and healthy, thus preventing the risk of over-exhilaration.

The Importance of Pleasure: -
Having discussed the copulative role of the physical union, let us now direct our readers in the art of pleasure, for one cannot, and must not, exist without the other. Before undertaking the reproductive act husband and wife must prepare their bodies by bathing and, if possible, time their following embrace to follow directly after having had a warm shower or bath. This will have the most wonderfully warm effect upon their spirits. Once they have bathed, let the husband come to his wife in her private rooms.

Here, he must seek to entertain her, perhaps with wanton behaviour or gentle allurements to sexual copulation and all kinds of dalliances he might invent for her benefit. If she should appear to be cold to his advances or slow to turn her mind towards the act of love, he must embrace, tickle and cherish her. On no account should he attempt to abruptly break into the physical act, for this will cause her womb to be suddenly and dangerously distended. Rather, by intermixing wanton words and speeches with more wanton kisses, he shall encourage her little by little. He might pay attention to her secret parts, stroking and caressing them so that she may become more inclined towards the act of love.

If he is successful in this, at length her womb will strive and wax fervent, soon making both aware of its desire to cast forth its own seed. It is a well-known fact that the greater a woman's desire to engage in the reproductive act, the greater still will be her chances of conception. We would advise the couple that, during the heat of their embrace, there is no greater pleasure for husband and wife than to look most ardently into the gaze of his or her beloved and the position most equal to the enjoyment of this pleasure is to face one another mouth to mouth.

The most advantageous time for love has been widely discussed by many of our great intellectuals. A French writer of great celebrity has suggested that morning is the most desirable time for copulation as it is the spring of the day when all the functions of the physical man are renovated from his nightly rest. As far as our own mature opinion should be concerned or consulted in this matter, we would consider that the secrecy and quietude of the night would offer the moments most congenial to the gratification of a couple's mutual love. Night is often suggested to be the most proper time, yet it is also well known that society will find little offence in children begat in fields in the daytime, offspring who often become both fine and handsome.

For those couples for whom the bloom of youth has begun to fade, the art of love is still a most welcome act. It has been suggested that the reproductive instinct which drives the act of copulation ceases at the '*turn of life*', that period in a women's aging when she no longer menstruates. Yet we find that the evidence for this is in the contrary and it can be their desire for passion that is often increased in this period and continues in a lesser or greater degree to an extreme age.

A word of warning here to our most amorous couples: do not enjoy the act of copulation too much. Once a week is most sufficient to all needs; any more than this can result in children who are seen to be both sickly and weak. In all things we would happily invite you to live well, but to always enjoy your pleasures in moderation. Any over-exertion in this regard will only result in a seed altogether utterly incapable of the great work of generation. Men who too frequently indulge in the art of copulation will only cast forth a seed that is thin, raw and crudely undigested. The same result can be found in women, as do we not know that public women, those whom respectable women do not acknowledge, rarely conceive. This is due to a greatly weakened state of their genital system, induced solely by the too frequent indulgence in promiscuous intercourse.

We must also suggest to our readers that they allow the desire for copulation to grow naturally, never by demand or provocation. Whilst both day and night can arouse the sexual urges, for those who wish to conceive it is most advisable to embrace before the husband and wife rise in the morning, as then their natures will be unwearied from the duties of the day and the wife will not find it an inconvenience to lie quietly once her husband has left the marital bed.

Pregnancy: -

Once the pleasure of the physical act has yielded a successful result and the masculine and feminine seeds have combined to form a child, the thoughts of the couple will turn to the conditions most assured to result in a healthy and lengthy pregnancy. Although we know that it is the man who is the principal mover and causer of generation, once the act has finished we must acknowledge that it becomes the office of the mother to whom the child most owes their life and care as they grow within the womb. To secure a healthy pregnancy we offer this advice: if the woman is fruitful, let her make regular time for the gentle exercise of her muscles. Idleness is hateful in all forms and most destructive to the success of creation. This is the reason why women who live idly and fill their days with few activities have so little joy in the reproductive act. It is the happiness of poor men and women to be blessed with many children who are both strong and lusty; this comes directly from the labour in which their parents have found daily fulfilment.

When exercising, the mother must take special caution to avoid any frightful objects coming before her gaze. How fearful it is for her companions to be the painful witnesses to a sight which they know will wreak havoc on the unborn child. It is a serious social evil to allow deformed beggars to roam the streets and frighten pregnant women into giving birth to similarly shaped creatures. This terrifying fact is best known to medical men, for if it was public knowledge we would imagine that legislative steps would have most certainly been taken to prevent the risks involved in the public appearance of such individuals.

At all times must the sight of the mother be met with wondrous and goodly things, as this can only result in a beautiful and fair child in birth. When born, any defect in copulation will also be clearly apparent and will then be evident in the mind and temper of the child as it ages. As a hint hitherto, a child that was begat upon a set of stairs is most likely to be born with a crooked back and given in no small way to the fault of staring.

Whilst these are the considerations one must take into account in the design of the surroundings of the mother, there is nothing more destructive to the creation of beautiful offspring than the defects of a licentious parentage. The danger of a polluted father, who through illicit dalliances has sacrificed his health to some wanton individual, brings nothing but horror to the marital bed. His refusal to take the precautionary measures clearly advised for the prevention of infection by the learned authorities in this volume, subject not only himself to a disease and wasting of the genital organs, but his wife too. He has cheated her, and their line, of any suitable offerings at the nuptial altar.

If the forgiving, yet misguided wife should choose to allow the absent and polluted husband to return to her arms, she will only be able to conjure a weak and wretched offspring from their embrace. The children resulting from a union such as this will never be happy. Licentious behaviour must be checked by marriage, for a *hankering* for stimulants, such as spirits, opium and tobacco, is merely a passion acquired by habit. It does not follow the natural passions of thirst, hunger, the desire to urinate, etc. For the success of a family line, for joy to be found in the marital bed, libertine persuasions must be replaced with a dedication to the bonds of man and wife.

We are saddened to report to our readers that some men indulge in the habits that pollute them before they have decided to enter into the marriage state and in this regard, to those unfortunate beings we would recommend the use of contraceptive checks. We would consider it a crime most outrageous to bring into the world any human beings who are doomed, solely by the fault of their parentage, to an eternal misery or untimely and premature death. It is of great benefit that mankind has at his disposal ways that allow him to limit, at will, the number of his offspring. And greater still, that it is possible to do so without sacrificing the pleasure that attends the gratification of the sexual instinct. We think it a most worthy and moral practice to prevent the conception of any child, who, after it is born, would be in danger of murder by want of food, air, clothing or ill health, brought on solely by the polluted nature of its father or mother.

There is much that can be done to ensure that the child has a strong constitution. We hold great faith in the old adage that those children begat with the wind blown from the North are always stronger than those whose conception occurred during a wind which blows from the East. This easterly wind is much cooler and greatly detrimental to the success of copulation. If the conjoined parties wish to influence the complexion of their future progeny, we suggest that those children who are begotten in the spring and summertime are for the most part of a darker complexion than those begat in the winter months.

For those who indulge in the pleasures for the flesh outside of the bonds of marriage, generally speaking we observe there to be a great tendency for an illegitimate child to be surprisingly full of fire and energy. This is evidence of the passions which took hold of their parents at the time of their conception, as they would not have been of a sleepy or considered nature.

Once the lengthy months of pregnancy have passed and the fully formed child reaches the time of its arrival, we have some small words of consultation to offer to those women who are moved to great pain or intolerable anguish during the time of their travail. It is not uncommon for them to forswear forever the future company of men and vow that they shall never seek the union of the flesh again. We assure all worried parties that within a short while, and after the pangs are over, they forget the sorrows that have just passed. Whether it is the arrival of a new and wholly innocent life; the entire and complete love of their husbands; or the desire of the singular natural delight between man and woman, husband and wife, the marriage union is soon renewed. It must always be borne in mind that the divine working and urgings of nature have never created any special pleasure or moment of great joy, which is not accompanied in equal measure by some small amount of sorrow.

Family Life: -

Now married life will begin in earnest, as the joys of natural love have been recognised and the act of generation seen to be a success. We have a few words of caution to exercise those young couples, heady with the bountiful gifts bestowed on them in the early years. A wise man once said, '*When poverty comes in the door, Love flies out the window*' and we would urge our readers to take heed of this most important of mottos. It would be well for all concerned that the solemn obligations of the married state are most deeply impressed upon the minds of a young couple, ere they take to themselves a partner for life. We must leave lovers to dwell on romance and moonshine, for a married couple must have bread and butter, a home furnished with linen and chairs, and the ability to pay the butcher's bills. Foolish poetic ideas that love is increased by a bare cupboard or the surroundings of poverty are to be discouraged. Love is the most sustainable of emotions and we can well exist on it as long as we have the addition of three meals a day, a good home and the timely addition of something most lovable to cherish.

Once the early mist of wedded bliss has passed, there is a danger that the monotonous realities of married life can be a sobering process. It may bring vertigo, or a type of weariness to one or both of the couple, and people who are miserable in each other's company constantly would believe themselves to be far happier when only occasionally together. At this point, often a marriage is beset by arguments and dissatisfaction, but it would do well for all to remember that calm and reasonable people are well able to agree to disagree and avoid that highly senseless folly of pressing upon their beloved the importance of their own notions. This, we believe, would be the secret of a happy and lengthy marriage.

We would also recommend that husbands and wives do not always desire to be constantly together. A daily separation is best and is often universally provided by the working day. In some cases, even a weekly separation may be sought, for as we enjoy a beautiful and engaging picture when it is not always within our sight, the same can be said of marriage. The most loving of couples must, for their own sakes, ensure that they enjoy the occasional interval of separation to felicitate matrimonial harmony. If they are not loving towards each other, then the longer the interval, the better.

Divorce: -

Which brings us to our most modern ideas for the marital union, that of the question of divorce. It is a harsh reality of our modern world that divorces seem to become more numerous every year. There are conflicting ideas on the matter at hand and its impact on the reputations of those involved. All we advise in this matter is the exercise of each individual's own common sense. Why should two persons find themselves to be made wretched for life by being compelled to live together if their union is found to have been a hasty or rushed decision? It would seem to be a most terrible punishment for a youthful error in judgement.

Why should they not be granted a divorce? Or take the case of a newly discovered flaw in one or other of the couple. And what about a systematic and brutal cruelty; persistent neglect of the home and children; a sudden revelation of habitual drunkenness or any form of malicious persecution? Surely these also seem to supply ample grounds for divorce. But our laws demand the degradation of one party by the other and the committal of an act of illicit connection with another person outside of the marriage bed for a divorce to be granted. This is a most antiquated view and we would argue that a divorce should, in any truly and properly civilised country, be granted on the proof of persistent evidences of incompatibility presented by both husband and wife. No court in the land should deny such a dissolution if it is thoughtfully and mutually asked for.

We all hope that when husband and wife are enjoined in the marital union they will continue to learn to love one another and that such a love will see a growth and a deepening as the years pass. If they cannot find success in this they should be legally allowed to separate without the required degradation of the marriage vows as asked for by our system of law. It is most distressing that even in France, where divorces are not allowed, separation *is* permitted to an understanding and agreeable couple without a shameful reputation being attached to those involved, but no marriage to another party is legal whilst either husband or wife is still alive. This system carries its own flaws and yet we would prefer it to our own.

And it is there that we shall leave our advice for marital relations and hope that it has been both an aid and a balm to those for whom it was intended. Remember, dear Readers, husband and wife together are as the stars and moon in firmament of the heavens; without one, the other is incomplete. He may rule by day and she may rule by night, yet they must be one in all things. Marriage is a union of two opposing forces and now, we would hope, our Readers will have at their disposal the tools with which to make all of its joys and sorrows a success.

Volume 5

Mr. Mandrake's Compendium of Practical Aids

Pills and Solutions: Gleet – Gonorrhoea – Syphilis – Spermatorrhoea –
Sterility – Painful Menstruation – A Test for Pregnancy –
Vomiting during Pregnancy – Hysteria.

Devices: The Condom – The Dildoe – The Ladies Syringe – The Veedee
Vibrator – Vigor's Horse-Action Saddle – The Femme de Voyage
and its Origin – Preventative Rings

For those of a discerning and curious nature, the sexual experience of the human being is often one of great interest and so a chemist's position in life, such as my own, is not one of moral judgement. After advice has been sought from the prevalent medical authorities, it is my role to dispense – to both individuals and doctors alike – the best cures or treatments available to aid in the fight against their current bodily distresses.

I have, within my wide collection, cures and comforts for all diseases that can be collected in the recourse of sexual misadventure. And for those of a truly enquiring mind and most discreet nature, I am able to furnish you with the practical devices most helpful in matters of a sexual and medicinal nature. My compendium is one of a truly unique standard – there is not another like it in the world and I am most grateful for your discerning perusal of the said articles, information about which is held within the following pages.

Gleet: -

'An inflammation of the urethra, causing itching and a pus or mucous to appear from the male genital organ, with pain during urination.'

Although harmless in appearance and often ignored by patient and doctor alike, *gleet* is a universal symptom of an underlying and poorly treated case of the clap. I have seen *gleet* itself refered to as 'chronic clap'; by the French it is known as '*Goutte militaire*'; by the Germans, '*Nachtripper*'. Although not infectious in itself, *gleet* is symptomatic of a deeper infection within the patient – one who has indulged in either too much wine or too many women. Often the appearance of *gleet* has caused an unwise husband to accuse his wife or mistress of having infected him with *gonorrhoea*. This is a mistake on his part as the disease of *gleet* comes from within the man himself.

There are a number of treatments available to remove the discharge caused by inflammation of the male urethra: -

Alteratives: - Iodine; iron; electricity applied to the local or infected area of the body; violent exercise; and injections of Zinc Sulphate, or bicholride of mercury, or nitrate of silver.

Specifics: - Balsam; capaivae; cubebs; turpentine Peruvian Balsam; Juniper Oil; Sandalwood Oil.

Tonics: - Bark; red wine to be imbibed and also as an injection; sea bathing; cold bathing.

Astringents: - iodine of iron; perchloride of iron; lead, Zinc Sulphate (in mild form); injection of nutgall and injection of chloride of lime.

All will be available to you from a chemist's dispensary or by a doctor's recommendation. Should you feel unable to visit either, you can always purchase a box of '*Holyroyd's Gravel Pills*', a well-known cure-all for infection of the urinary organs. Price is 1s 1½d, if obtained from a chemist's, or on receipt of 18 stamps to Holyroyd's Medical Hall, Cleckton, Yorkshire. Don't be put off; embarrassment must never stand in the way of good health.

Gonorrhoea: -

'An infection of the genital organs, appearing in both sexes, and capable of being transmitted between them, also known as the Clap.'

The manifestation of this disease has led to widespread discussions amongst the medical fraternity. Previously ignored by many medical men who were preoccupied with the control and cure of that most destructive of diseases – namely, *syphilis* – gonorrhoea has been regarded as being of lesser importance and so any investigation into the symptoms was passed over. However, with the great advances that have been made in this area in recent years, *gonorrhoea* has been identified as a disease that is most in need of combative medical actions.

Taking between three to five days to incubate within the body after infection, the first symptoms of the disease are a stinging or prickling sensation around the genital area and a slight reddening of the flesh. This is followed by a mucous pus-like secretion which gradually increases in colour and texture over the coming weeks. The genitals will deepen in their inflammation, but at the end of the third week all symptoms will seem to decrease in severity. In certain cases, the irritation caused by the inflammation will have led to continual and painful erections for male sufferers, but this is not a universal symptom. Bed rest is the most important stage of treatment for a sufferer, with no physical activity of any kind to be attempted until all symptoms have passed. Other useful treatments are as follows: -

Acid, Boric
Acid, Camphoric
Acid, Gallic
Acid, Tannic
Alcohol is not to be touched
Belladonna
Cinnamon Oil
Cocaine: as an injection to relieve the pain
Lead Water and Laudanum
Silver Nitrate: as an injection
Urinating: with penis in hot water to relieve pain
Warm Baths: lasting ¼ to 2 hours, in the early stages of the infection
Zinc Salts in general.

Syphilis: -

This scourge of humankind is vulgarly known as the '*Pox*' and its origin is clouded in mystery. Some believe it first appeared in Spain, others assert France. I consider the disease to have emerged with the origin of mankind. Modern syphilis has been established to appear in three separate stages: primary, secondary and tertiary. The first symptoms will make their appearance on the genital organs about three to four weeks after infection. This is due to the difficulty of washing thoroughly this area of the body and after a filthy connection the poison is apt to lodge in the folds of the skin of the delicate parts of both men and women.

The first symptom is an itching, followed by a redness of the parts, from which is observed to spring a small pimple or elevation. These, in time, will turn into ulcerated lesions which if left untreated will attack the organs and bones of the human body, destroying them. One of the greatest tragedies of such a disease is the ability for the infected parent to pass on the illness to an unborn child. Children born with congenital syphilis often exhibit deformities and malformations and suffer greatly during their life, a life which will be significantly shortened by the disease.

As with many sexual diseases, the curative treatments for *syphilis* are wide-ranging and often obtainable. Yet one treatment above all is seen as to be successful and that is the application of mercury:

Rules for the Application of Mercurial Ointments:
1. Every night the patient must take a warm bath for 15 minutes.
2. Rub a piece of ointment, as large as the last joint of the forefinger, into some part of the body every night with the palm of the hand, for a quarter of an hour.
3. The ointment is to be rubbed into one of the following places: - Inner side of the thighs, avoiding the groins; sides of the chest, avoiding the hairy armpits; inner surfaces of arms and forearms; buttocks; back or belly.
4. Never rub into the same place two nights running.
5. After rubbing in the ointment, leave it without washing any off until the next bath.
6. Clean teeth twice a day.

Rules for the Injection:
1. Get a glass syringe that holds about four teaspoonfuls of the mercury solution and has a bulbous end.

2. Urinate and inject in some tepid water before using the mercury injection, so as to clean and clear the passage.

3. Inject so as to distend the urine canal, and let the injection stay in half a minute. Do this twice each time.

4. Repeat the injection each time before making water, except at bedtime.

5. The injection may be weakened by the addition of water when the discharge has ceased and gradually discontinued.

N.B. Every patient must keep his person thoroughly clean by washing with soap and water every day.

Spermatorrhoea: -

The dangers associated with the seminal loss arising from masturbation have been discussed in other volumes; here I will only set out those methods most relied upon to treat this disease of men. Persons who are very sensitive nervously, and especially Americans, are liable to develop all or many of the symptoms of sexual nervous exhaustion, or *spermatorrhoea*, due to the stimulants of work, worry, tobacco, alcohol, trauma or excess.

There are three methods of treatment available to the sufferer: first, general or constitution treatment; second, local or medical treatment; third, surgical treatment. The majority of cases do not need to resort to the third and final option.

1. *General Treatment:* routine work, travel, massage and marriage.

2. *Medical treatment:* Digitalis, Camphoric Acid, Belladonna: to aid in the relaxation of the genital organs where there is no dream or orgasm; one-fourth grain of extract, and a grain and a half of zinc sulphate; Bladder to be emptied as soon as the patient wakes; Electricity: one electrode is placed near the rectum and the other near the urethra, a *very mild* current to be passed between them; Use of a spinal ice bag.

3. *Surgical Treatment:* Removal of the foreskin has some surgical success as it decreases the sensitivity of the male genital organ.

Sterility: -

This is a most delicate and painful of problems to arise from the genital organs. A simple list of treatments follows, as your doctor will best guide you in the maintenance of a healthy diet and vigorous exercise.

Alkaline Injections: in excessively acid secretions from the vagina.
Borax: vaginal injections in acid secretions.

Cantharides: as a stimulant where there is impotence in either sex.
Electrical Stimulation of the uterus.
Key-tsi-ching: a Japanese remedy for male sterility.
Phosphorus: functional debility in the male.

Painful Menstruation: -

Plenty of healthy exercise is recommended in these cases and riding especially will promote the circulation through the pelvis and give the generative organs a better chance of developing fully in youth, thereby greatly reducing any further pain. The diet should be wholesome. During the pain most patients improve with rest, even bed rest, but some find relief with active exercise.

Pessaries are absolutely useless and amongst the drugs that are of benefit, guaiacum mixed with or without sulphur and taken regularly in milk is a common aid. Castoreum oil has sometimes been known to banish the spasms felt within the uterus completely: give, in a tincture, from 20 to 30 drops three or four times daily during the pain. Old home remedies include a hot footbath and decent glass of hot gin-and-water at bedtime. Ergot, another useful tonic to ease the spasms, is a small pill made from the syrup of poppies, taken in the morning and in the evening during the menstrual flow.

A Test For Pregnancy: -

A new and ingenious test for pregnancy was reliably discovered by our American friends in 1844. They have found that the urine of a pregnant woman contains a particular and unique substance and have named this '*Kisteine*'. When the urine is left to stand it will separate and form a thin layer on the surface. This will only appear if the urine is left undisturbed for between two to six days. During this time minute opaque bodies will be observed to rise from the bottom to the surface of the fluid, where they gradually combine to form a continuous layer over the surface. This is the '*Kisteine*' and will only appear to exist in the urine from the first month of pregnancy until the woman has safely delivered her child.

Vomiting During Pregnancy: -

Known as the dreaded '*morning sickness*', the arrival of vomiting is one of the most unfortunate symptoms of the pregnant state and it is one of those situations that medicine has commonly failed to relieve. Cures renowned to ease the suffering of one woman will often do little to aid another. I have this simple piece of advice to offer: a cup of chamomile or peppermint tea should be taken on first waking. The patient should then be entreated to be still for an hour. This method has had the most success in alleviating the distressing sickness, but should it appear during the day, then any selected treatment seldom succeeds.

Hysteria: -

The cure of this illness can be found in manifold supply. However, for as many legitimate and reputable treatments that might be discussed, there can equally be found those of a dangerous and damaging nature which are promoted by quacks and charlatans.

'Full Current', c. early 1900s, (Library of Congress).

There is only one certain cure, acknowledged by all to remove the symptoms of this illness: **Massage.** This is the most beneficial treatment and one which I will set out in detail. It can be performed either by hand, or with the aid of devices, the details of which will also follow on for the Reader's benefit and perusal. But what IS *Hysteria?* Its symptoms are many, its causes limitless, and, in some circles, it is no longer regarded as solely the women's disease – having been found to occur in nervous young men of a weakened constitution. For a most detailed analysis of the disease I turn to that new and modern magazine, *Hearth and Home,* for a discussion of the case in question:-

Hysteria may be defined as an imperfect power to control the emotional functions. This may be due to a weakness of the nerves, or the result of a sudden nervous shock; but it is in many cases due to a want of will power. Does a low and weak condition of the body have any effect upon this weakness of the nerves or will? Yes, we can safely say it does, for the close intimacy of the physical functions with the nervous system is apparent.

A sudden mental shock or any depression of the mind is also a great strain upon the body; therefore we expect to find that in cases of prolonged grief or worry the body will get into a low debilitated state. As a rule, in nervous and hysterical patients the appetite altogether departs. It becomes necessary then to administer a concentrated form of nourishments, which will enable the body to withstand the strain imposed upon it, and at the same time strengthen the nerves. It cannot be denied that the absence of any definite occupation plays a most important part in these cases. Healthy outdoor recreation should be taken by those of hysterical tendency, such games as croquet, lawn tennis, etc., being most beneficial.

We must distinguish between the 'hysterical fit' which commences with crying or laughing and ends in utter convulsion and the many deceptive acts which are often perpetrated by silly women who wish to excite sympathy. When a woman is hysterical the first thing to do is to remove all sympathizing friends, loosen all tight garments, and treat her firmly but considerately. We frequently find other disturbances of the nervous system associated with hysteria, notably neuralgic pains which generally cease when the nerves are strengthened with a course of the medicine mentioned above. Stimulants should never be administered in cases of hysteria, a douche of cold water being generally sufficient to arouse the patient. If this should fail - and it seldom does - medical aid should be sought as it may become necessary to administer chloroform. An examination of the blood of a hysterical patient shows it to be deficient in the normal quality of iron. This, if it be the case, will show itself in the pale bloodless cheeks and lips, the dull eye, and the general want of 'go'. To remedy this, two bisalatinoids of carbonate of iron three times a day directly after meals will quickly supply the deficiency.

Much hysterical behaviour can be dealt with in the home, without the need to call a doctor, thereby distressing the patient further. A well regarded method follows that the person in question should be quickly separated from their family – especially their mother – lain on a waterproof sheet on the floor, and, after the first symptoms of an hysterical attack having been witnessed, quickly doused with a jug of cold water. Should this be unsuccessful, I would advise you to immediately call a doctor. Once the hysterical fit has passed, the patient will be left feeling somewhat weak and listless. To quickly remedy this and return their constitution to a healthy and vibrant peak, I can recommend nothing better than a tablespoon of *Cream of Malt* with Cod Liver Oil and Hypophosphites, taken directly after meals, and continued for two or three weeks. A list of other useful tonics will always include: -

Alcohol
Anesthetics
Arsenic
Belladonna
Camphor: to be taken in Hysterical Excitement
Cocaine Hydrochlorate
Cod Liver Oil
Cold Water: poured over mouth to cut short attack
Electricity: to cut short attack
Ether
Garlic: to smell during the paroxysm
Massage
Musk
Opium: in small doses

As I have previously said, massage is a treatment which is applicable to many ailments. In many diseases of the nervous system it is invaluable and none more so in the treatment of those with *Hysteria*. The performance of a medicinal massage is not a difficult task and can soon be learnt by any person with a steady head on their shoulders. In its most simple and direct form, massage consists of rubbing in the direction of circulation. There are many more elaborate manoeuvres, purportedly offered by bathing houses and institutes specialising in forms of water cure, but these are not often necessary, nor are they always beneficial. Often the massages in such establishments will require considerable skill, and so must only ever be performed by a professional nurse. But do not despair! Not every symptom of hysteria denotes a severe case so simple home massage is up to the task of relieving many a sufferer of their troubles.

Do not be delicate in your approach to the task at hand. Massage does not consist of gentle rubbing; it must be carried out by a concentrated and determined touch. You must massage firmly. However, make sure to begin lightly and then gradually increase the firmness of the pressure until you are really rubbing very hard. As *The Girls Own Paper* reminds us,

> *the point is to rub with the finger-tips only; do not use your whole hand for the purpose. In some forms of massage the palm or the back of the hand is used; but for ordinary massage the fingers only should be used. Always rub towards the heart, rub firmly, and only rub with your fingers. When you are firmly rubbing a part which is normally hairy, you are likely to pull out sundry hairs, and so cause your patient considerable pain, and not unlikely the loss of their temper. This objection may be averted by dipping the tips of your fingers in sweet oil. The oil renders your fingers less likely to pull out hairs; but it also makes the massage rather more difficult, for the oiled fingers are apt to slip.*

Leaving you now equipped with the relevant methods, pills and solutions for all your aliments, the remainder of this compendium is preoccupied with the practical devices most able to aid you in the passionate nature of sexual relations. Remember, these are only for those of a discreet nature. Their manufacturers and distributors must at all times ensure that no impropriety can be attached to their name or reputation.

The Condom or Baudruche: -

The most trustworthy artificial protective measure in modern society against the fears of unwarranted pregnancy and pollution is also the oldest: *The Condom*. When of a good quality, applied with care and removed delicately, there is little to surpass its effectiveness. Only the male, who makes use of it to cover his penis, wears this device. When properly placed, the condom will protect both man and woman from infection and the risks of pregnancy. Little is known about the origins or invention of the device, though authorities from the very beginning of our great century claim that it was invented by Colonel Cundum, of the guards, in the time of Charles II – a somewhat dubious assertion.

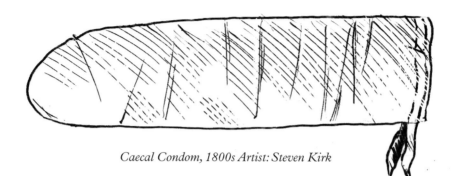

Caecal Condom, 1800s Artist: Steven Kirk

The traditional condom is also known as a *Baudruche* although this word has fallen increasingly out of use as our century comes to a close. It is a 'caecal' condom, made from the mucous intestinal organ of either a goat or a sheep. This material is preferred by all who are acquainted with the device, as it is lighter and more delicate than other fabrics, thereby leading to increased sensation. Another favourable quality is that they can be made by the most uneducated of housewives, following these simple instructions:

Take the caecum of the sheep; soak it first in water, turn it on both sides, then repeat the operation in a weak solution of soda, which must be changed every four to five hours, for four to six successive times; then remove the mucous membrane with the nail; rub with sulpher, wash in clean water, and then in soap and water; rinse, inflate and dry. Next cut it to the required length, and attach a piece of ribbon to the open end. The different qualities consist in extra pains being taken in the above process, and in polishing, scenting &c.

Should you not wish to undertake the manufacturing process yourself, caecal condoms are the most expensive of design to purchase. They are available from discerning individuals, such as myself, and often stocked by the matrons in charge of houses of disrepute. The ability for caecal condoms to be designed for the specifications of an individual wearer, as well as the unique opportunity for scenting and decorating the object in mind has led to an advertising boom which, I have heard, includes the placement of the portrait of widely renowned and celebrated personages on the front!

The only failure of this first design is its delicate and fragile nature, which is apt to break and tear during vigorous use. The more modern designs are made of rubber – either gutta-percha or caoutchouc – and are far more durable and resistant to tearing than those made of animal gut. Their trustworthiness, however, does in turn lead to a more noticeable loss of sensation. They are less likely to decay if the owner takes care to keep them in a cool place, rather than carrying them in the pocket where they are prone to damage and likely to tear due to the continual warmth. This protective measure is agreed upon as the very best surety against infection from either *gonorrhoea* or *syphilis* and one suggested by all leading physicians who specialise in the treatment of venereal disease.

The Dildoe: -

The artificial imitation of the male penis is an old and substantial art form, with examples believed to have been found in ancient Babylonian sculpture, Eastern Asia, and the classical poetry of Greece. In the eleventh century, the writer of *Decretum*, the Bishop Burchard of Worms, was forced to include directions for those listening to a confession of the use of such instruments. Their design and appearance can take many forms, being made variously from wood, ivory, metal, glass, wax or rubber. This is by no means a completed list, but rather examples of possible materials.

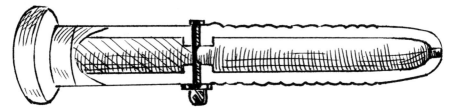

Dildoe: Artist: Steven Kirk

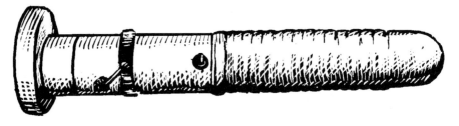

They are known by many names: *godemiche*, *dildoe* and *consolateurs* being the most common. The word itself is believed to be from either the Italian *'Diletto'* to mean a 'woman's delight', or the English word *'dally'* to mean a thing to play with. Although not a device favoured for medical treatment, it is one that is a source of great physical pleasure and so I have included it herein, for those who are so inclined.

I have in my collection, and available for purchase, a highly artistic object –

a dildoe made from the best quality ivory, patiently carved with circular ridges that extend horizontally down the shaft and known to provide the most enjoyable sensations. But these decorations are not what make this design so remarkable. It is the internal mechanics of the article concerned which elicit the greatest wonderment. Located near the base, a small screw extends away from the shaft, the head of which is flattened. When this is rotated, it allows an internal divider to move within the device, which is in itself hollow. The base of the dildoe is formed of a detachable plug, also carved from ivory, and when removed reveals a small space which can be filled with warm water. The plug is replaced and at a timely moment, the catch can be turned to mimic the male ejaculation. This is a most rewarding feature of the modern design.

Words of caution now to those of you who indulge in the use of such devices. I have been informed that hairpins, lead and slate pencils, leather thongs, sealing wax and other like substances have been used in the past as substitutions for the investment of a manufactured apparatus. But these carry with them great dangers, as small implements have been known to slip from the fingers of the operator into the vagina, where they remain to form a nuclei for cystic calculi and internal infections.

In Germany, the year of 1862 saw the ingenious invention by one determined surgeon of a special tool specifically designed for the removal of hairpins from the female bladder, as masturbation with such objects had become so common. It is clear that the introduction of foreign bodies, such as candles, stiff rubber tubes or dildoes, is done with the express desire of producing an artificial physical excitement. The loudest authorities of our day would insist that such actions are the concerns of masturbators, and risk all the diseases with which that term is associated. But a most recent publication in 1899, namely, the *American Journal of Obstetrics*, has reported the case of a woman who indulged in the act as it provided her with immediate relief of intense menstrual pains. The father of phrenology, Franz Joseph Gall, was also aware of its ability to reduce pain, so with the voices of two such authorities, one from the beginning of our century and one from the end, how can I argue against such benefits?

The Ladies Syringe: -

The most reliable design, made from a material of the latest fashion is the rubberised '*Ladies Syringe*'. It is the only example, from which there are a plethora of styles and materials, that I would be inclined to recommend to you. I have included herein an account from its manufacturer, which will answer any questions you might desire to ask on design, function and durability.

The Dildoe, or Ladies Syringe

The grand desideratum accomplished by the Patentee, is the substitution of Indian-Rubber for the shaft of this article, instead of ivory, wood, silver, wax, or porcelain, heretofore used, none of which substances could resemble the real thing in effect, however beautiful they might be shaped and painted. The Indian-Rubber shaft, when dipped in warm water to bring it to blood heat, sufficiently soft and elastic to titillate the female seat of pleasure, without excoriating the vagina, or injuring the mouth of the uterus.

The most complete article is made with a stomacher, in order that one female may fix it firmly on herself so as to operate upon another female. In this case, the ball, or scrotum, is placed between the thighs of the Operator. The upper strings are passed around her waist, and tied in front; and the under strings round the thick part of the thighs and tied behind. In this manner the machine will remain firm and effective through the 'soft encounter,' and the receiving female is wrought to that delightful pitch of burning ecstasy until she requires the balmy shower of love to consummate her bliss. She need only to say 'NOW!' and the Operator can instantly produce the exhilarating injection by nipping the scrotum with her thighs, because the ball being previously charged with water, only requires a slight pressure to produce that thrilling sensation so much desired at the critical moment.

This noble instrument may justly be entitled the Maid's Safeguard, the Widow's Comfort, and the Wife's Consolation.

It will cure the virgin of the green sickness with the risk of impregnation. It will comfort the widow until she can make a suitable match. And it will be found a never-failing source of consolation to those married ladies whose husbands are impotent thro' age or debauchery.

Many elderly gentlemen, whose affairs have shrunk into their bellies, are in the habit of strapping these devices on, in order to administer due benevolence to the aged partner of their beds, because it is well known that a woman is never too old to relish enjoyment although age incapacitates the male from performing the operation.

Directions for use – Put a little soap and water into a jug, then take the article and dip its head in, pressing the ball with the thumb, when it will immediately fill. Before using put a lather of soap and water on the head; after using, squeeze out all of the contents, and hang it up to dry, with the head downwards. Use the water tolerably warm, and take care not to put pomatum, or grease of any kind upon it, as it softens it too much, and causes it to assume a white colour, which cannot be got out.

Price from £5 to £20.

The VeeDee Vibrator: -

The newest device availed to those in need of hysterical and muscular relief is the '*VeeDee Vibrator*'. This is the most modern of inventions, available only at select chemists, and I predict it will become all the rage for the coming century. Manufactured by Mr. J.E. Garret of 96 Southwark Street, London, the *VeeDee Vibrator* can be used as a cure-all for muscular pain, problems of the circulation and, most importantly, as a practical aid for those ladies suffering from the symptoms of debilitating nervous diseases and *hysteria*. Massage, especially that which comes with mechanical relief, has been shown to give rapid relief from the symptoms of hysteria that so torments such a large proportion of the women in this country.

The *VeeDee Vibrator* is constructed with a wooden handle, a metal shaft with a circular disk and multiple attachments. Turning the handle in an anticlockwise direction will allow the flat metal disk at the top to spin. The vibration of this carries down the shaft to the arm, which has been attached below the flat disk, on which a small metal cup has been secured to the end. Held within this cup is a small hollow ball and it is this attachment that we see most commonly used for muscular aid. The vibration travels down the arm into the hollow ball, which rotates and spins, thus creating the vibrating and soothing sensation.

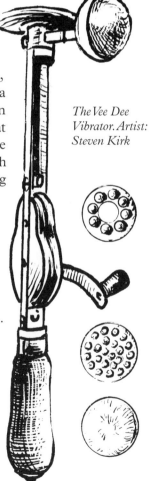

The Vee Dee Vibrator. Artist: Steven Kirk

One of the advantages of the *VeeDee Vibrator*'s modern capabilities is that it comes with a number of attachments to provide its owner with varied sensations. From different sized balls to flat rubber discs, to rubber pointed attachments of a stippling sensation, there can also be included attachments of a cylindrical and rounded nature for use in extreme cases of hysteria. Unlike earlier designs, the *VeeDee* requires no batteries or electrical stimulation. It is a simple system of automated machine manipulation, which can be operated very easily by its owner.

Such devices are not a wholly new invention to the world of women's medicine. Dr. Joseph Mortimer Granville, who first patented the automated vibration device in 1883, describes the correct use of vibration machines as being the repeated performance of '*a particular set of automatic movements as many as four or five times in succession, with intervals of ten or fifteen seconds, by a few minutes' vibration'.*

Vigor's Horse-Action Saddle: -

Available from Vigor & Co., 21 Baker Street, Portman Square, London, the 'Hercules' model of their original design, *'The Horse-Action Saddle'* has been widely available since 1885. The mechanical exercise device has been constructed to mimic the movements and effects of riding a horse. Built to occupy no more space than the dimensions of a saddle, this device will fit comfortably into any home. It has a number of unique advantages, being a sure substitute for horse riding and possessing the singular quality of inexpensive maintenance – compared with the live animal – as well as the ability to be ridden indoors. It is a remarkably beneficial machine for those who seek to create appetite, quicken their own circulation and most importantly of all, to aid in the treatment of that most distressing of diseases, and one to which both men and women can fall prey:- *Hysteria.*

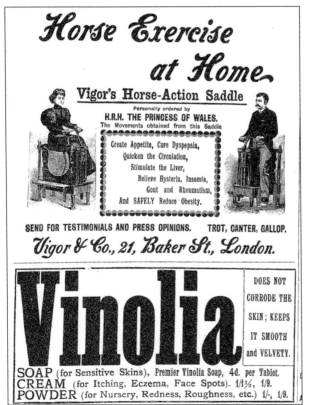

The Graphic, 29 June 1895.

Symptoms will find immediate relief after you simply seat yourself upon the contraption, either astride, or side-saddle, as you would on a real horse, not forgetting to tightly clench the muscles to ensure you have a good purchase on the device. Holding on to the handles in front of you, it is then possible to select the speed at which you wish the action to commence – trot, canter and gallop are all available. I recommend you remain atop the machine for as long as needed to create the desired reaction and relief from your symptoms.

Applications for testimonials and press opinions can be obtained from the address provided, but the knowledge that this device has been personally ordered by Her Royal Highness, Alexandra of Denmark, The Princess of Wales, is surely all the recommendation you will need. Her Excellency, Ishbel Hamilton-Gordon, Marchioness of Aberdeen and Temair writes that '*The Saddle has given her complete satisfaction*', and with such glowing reports from these guiding lights of society it is hardly unexpected that the medical community has followed suit. *The Lancet* review reads: - '*both the expense and difficulty of riding on a live horse are avoided. The invention is very ingenious.*' And those daring adventurers at Field's say: - '*We have had the opportunity of trying one of the* Vigor's Horse-Action Saddles, *and found it very like that of riding on a horse; the same muscles are brought into play as when riding.*' The final word on the subject must, of course, belong to those literary individuals at World: - '*It is very good for the* Figure, *good for the* Complexion, *and* Especially Good For The Health.'

The Femme de Voyage and its Origin: -

I will now draw your attention to this recent advertisement which I came across in a privately circulated magazine.

The Femme de Voyage or Artificial Fanny,

For the special use of Gentlemen on their travels. This can be packed up so as to be put in a hat, and when inflated, occupies the same space that the living object it is intended to represent would. They are made of all sizes, from the full-length figure, with all its appurtenances, to the small quartering containing only the essential part wanted by man.

Price from five to one hundred guineas.

I was immediately struck by the ingenious design of such an object as it seems to me to be a highly successful alternative to those who fear contamination or pollution from illicit acts with questionable lovers. As the *dildoe* provides necessary comfort to women, why should not the same artificial relief be found for men?

I have been told there is also available a '*Hommes de Voyage*' for ladies, built to represent the male form, but as much of the earlier passages of this volume have been devoted to objects for women, I feel duty bound to now discuss those specifically designed for men. Those who lust after the *tableaux vivants* of our variety theatres – the charmingly erotic nudes, standing immobile on the stage night after night to present some classical visage – will see them hereby made real, without the damage to a person's reputation that so often comes with a union of anyone from the stage profession. I am assured they are most realistic and entrancing in their feminine appearance, but the ingeniousness of such objects is their ability to be broken down into singular parts and thereby disguised from prying eyes and overly familiar servants.

Should you wish to invest in a full-scale model, the opportunities are there, but rather, if you seek a comforter to take on your travels there is the alternative to carry with you the most important part of the artificial women, cleverly disguised within a gentleman's top hat. Manufacturers for these objects can be found in catalogues purporting to be of '*Parisian Rubber Articles*'. Send your enquiries to such distributors and I am sure your acquisition will be a success. However, I must make you aware that these are articles for the connoisseur only, those with a considerable amount of disposable financial capital, as the cost of the *Femme de Voyage* is considerably out of the reach of most ordinary persons.

There has been published in the most recent of years an erotic novella called *La Femme Endormie* by the mysterious Madam B. In it, the heroine is herself an artificial woman, built for the purpose we have discussed. Although not widely available, this fiction takes its inspiration from the reality of the invention of the *Femme de Voyage*. One of the joys of experiencing life in our great age is the opportunity to see imagination become reality. Our inventions are shaping the modern world and I do not doubt that they will continue to do so.

Preventative Rings: -

Having explored those devices made for pleasure, I will now return to those of a medicinal nature. These special devices are commonly known as 'pollution rings' and are for use in the treatment of chronic masturbators or those who suffer with the deadly disease of *spermatorrhoea* and nightly emissions.

Believed to be of a German design originating in the 1870s, they encompass two nickel-plated metal rings, one internal and one external. The internal ring is made of two parts, which can be pulled apart so as to be fitted on to the main male organ of generation whilst it is in a relaxed state. The device will then be held there without interference from the second ring, until the wearer finds himself becoming aroused, either whilst he is awake, or whilst he is sleeping. Should he feel the urges of lust in a conscious moment, the knowledge of the second external ring and its effects will soon lead to a quick retraction of these feelings.

They are a certain and sure tool in teaching the individual the art of self-control. However, should this occur at night, whilst his mind is not troubled by the actions of the day, the second ring, with its circle of sharp, inward-pointing teeth, will quickly act as a deterrent to the wearer, often causing him to wake from the pain they will inflict upon his most sensitive part. As the organ swells the teeth will meet the skin, and create a most unpleasant sensation. Although this pain is unfortunate, it will stop the wearer from suffering the far more deadly effects of nightly emissions, protecting his sanity and good physical health. In most cases, I would recommend that they need be only used at night. I supply a number to doctors and individuals in London, both for private personal use, and for use on those poor souls confined within lunatic asylums. Often, one look at the device alone is enough to deter the most disobedient child or adult.

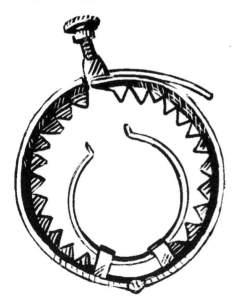

Anti Masturbation Device, 1870s onwards. Artist: Steven Kirk

The device you see illustrated overleaf is of a model from a slightly later design, the screw catch having been improved upon from an earlier innovation of a simple repeating hole lock. This new modernisation allows for greater alteration in tightness to suit the individual's needs and girth. I must offer a cautious counsel to any buyer against tightening the ring too greatly on first use, as the teeth can inflict serious damage on the wearer if the device is misused. This alteration to the design will allow you to pinpoint with greater accuracy the exact circumference needed to act as deterrent, without damage to your second most important organ – the first, of course, being one's mind. Through proper attention and under medical advisement, I believe pollution rings to be a most ingenious and successful solution to the disease of *spermatorrhoea*. I have heard suggestions that the device is of potential favour amongst those of a religious ilk. However, I would request most strongly that it is only ever to be used for medical matters and with the instruction of the proper authorities.

It has been theorised that there are those who see another use for these devices, one that turns pain into pleasure. I have a limited understanding of such actions, although I do believe there are greater authorities than myself within our illustrious society and perhaps it is to their knowledge you should now turn.

Lord Arthur Cleveland's Advice for Extreme Tastes

The Immoral Traffic of Girls Abroad – Prostitutes and Their Types –
The Dangers of Prostitution – Sappho and her Followers – Sodomites –
The Cleveland Street Scandal – Boarding School Boys –
A Breach of Promise – Brothels – The English Vice

I am a man of the world and make no apologies for having lived as one. I have never married and have therefore seen fit to indulge my passionate nature free of the fetters of marital duty. This is merely a record of my experiences, to be drawn on by those who seek guidance in such matters.

The Immoral Traffic of Girls Abroad: -

I have for some time past kept company at the house of Madam D'Alma, at 67 Newman Street, Marylebone, London. She was a most competent companion, although she has recently had to return to her native Paris due to certain difficulties created by her occupation. I thought little of her absence until hearing of the immoral traffic in young girls which has so preoccupied those investigative men and police of the city.

Imagine my surprise to find reports in the press that Mr. Albert, an agent of the Society for the Protection of Women and Children – which resides in Duke Street, St James, and of which Lord Rayham is president – had made an application to the Marlborough Street Police Court. The society had gone to great lengths to collect evidence to prove that young girls between the ages of 13 and 15 were regularly brought over from Belgium to London. The details of the particulars of these cases exposed an immoral traffic in young foreign women and stated that some of the girls were detained in the house of ill-fame against their will, then obliged to give themselves up to a life of prostitution!

Imagine my surprise at such shocking revelations! The reporting of young girls being brought over from Belgium, some under the pretence of being provided with situations, others without the knowledge and consent of their parents, and all compelled to enter upon a course of prostitution, is one seen in the pages of those unsuitable novels that young women are so prone to reading and which can lead only to the inducement of a hysterical fit. Clearly outraged, I read on. On arrival, the girls were supplied with clothes, jewellery and board, all at the houses' expense. Yet no matter how large the profits of their unhappy life, they were always said to be in debt. They were frequently beaten, confined to the house and ill-used in any manner of ways.

I thought of the time I had spent at Madam D'Alma's, then run by two charming French women – Clarissa Dorval, also known to many as Maria Cusho, and Athalie Vevey. I recalled them facing a somewhat similar investigation in 1870, being charged with keeping a common brothel – of little surprise to those in the locality as it had been operating as such for the previous ten years. They too kept a ready supply of Belgian women in work. Madam D'Alma's was set over four floors, three rooms on each, which were equipped with a bed alongside which had been fixed some looking glass lit with a gas chandelier. There was one sitting room, which upon entering I had found to hold nine immoral women, all most extravagantly dressed. The sitting room itself had a sofa, a couch and 14 chairs, and on the walls were nine looking glasses, also lit by gas chandeliers. Artificial flowers gave the most delightful dash of colour and were dotted around the room in a tasteful manner.

I believe when not entertaining gentlemen, the girls slept in rooms at the back of the house of a less opulent design, but I never ventured towards that portion. I had paid my gold sovereign on entering the house and would pay a further sovereign for the company of any lady I chose. This was a most

FOOD AND WATER ON THE WAY.

ALLEGED IMMORAL TRAFFIC IN CHINESE GIRLS.
THEY ARE PACKED IN CRATES AND TREATED AS FREIGHT ON THE RAILWAY.

Illustrated Police News, 17 June 1899

agreeable way to spend my time. What came of the investigation I do not recall, but I found instead my interest drawn to another case, much like the first, but this time reporting the distressing news that English girls were also being subjected to similar entrapments. Some girls, having taken positions with seemingly respectable men, were drugged and exported.

Another case saw the false adoptions of girls to men who then spirited these luckless innocents away and into the most horrifying of situations. Brussels saw the trial of 12 men in connection with the immoral trafficking of English girls, many of whom had been taken by force, and this has enabled the law to charge these evil individuals with the crime of kidnapping. It was only with the aid of two agents of the London Society for the suppression of this terrible industry, Mr. Alfred S. Dyer, of Paternoster Row, and Mrs. Steward, of Ongar, that the case was ever brought to court. It appears that the policemen of Brussels had previously accepted the word of the domestic servants in the houses where the girls were kept, and who acted as translators, conveying the girls' assertions that they were not kept there under duress. The exposé of such a practice was very damaging to the reputation of the police and the case created enough hue and cry to be brought before the court.

But such trafficking is not restricted to the fair city of London, or the Continent of Europe. In 1899 *The Illustrated Police News* carried within its pages such a black tale of deceit and enslavement as I have ever had the misfortune to read. In Vancouver, the shipment of Chinese girls in crates on board freight trains was a customary, although illegal, practice. The girls were packed into the crates and shipped from the seller to the procurer, surviving by being passed food and water by a sympathetic train hand. The practice only came to public attention when a crate carrying two young girls aged 15 and 16 was left overnight on a side track, and, being clad only in their day clothes, the girls both caught a violent chill. On the revelation of their illness, the man who had purchased one of them demanded damages from the railway company for the injury done to his property. This revealed the vile trade to the wider society and it has been widely condemned.

Prostitutes and Their Types: -

But what of those women who ply their wares in the industry known as 'The Great Social Evil' of our time, those without the assistance of a procurer, a seducer or madam? What of those ladies who walk the street, unfettered by the machine of industry that serves to traffic girls across continents, what of them I wonder? A man can find as many a loving companion on the street as he can in a privately held house and for far less damage to his purse. A girl on the street will be happy with a single shilling to pay for her services and a goodly sight more cheerful about the prospect.

But even here I find there exists the different orders. The women of the west of the great city of London are as different to those in the east as chalk is to cheese. In the West a woman is *joyous, juvenile and juicy*; fair and free. The neighbourhood off the Regent's Park and the streets diverging from the Edgeware Road will be her localities. Here these professors of voluptuous gymnastics will be flourishing and on those fine autumnal afternoons they may be seen airing themselves in the parks or walking down Regent Street, heavy in a toggery designed to allure and entice the amorous observer. Many of these 'unfortunate' creatures have been well educated and are connected, by birth, with most aristocratic families. This can make them occasionally difficult to detect from a truly virtuous lady. I would counsel a cautious approach on all occasions, as you would not wish to risk offering insult to any respectable woman. There are, however, some painted, silk-bedizened dolls who promenade the Haymarket and for all their finery are instantly known for their true purpose.

Now what of those glowering chits who stalk the Ratcliffe Highway? What a marked difference this feminine character has to her sister in the West. Those bejewelled butterflies appear quite frail in comparison to the Eastern beauties, who nightly prowl the docks and are known by that charming turn of phrase, 'Wapping Polls'. This East-Ender is far more dangerous than her western counterpart, being invariably in business for herself and operating under the motto that she will do '*nuffin for nothing for nobody*'. These enterprising ladies are not always devoted to the task at hand as their sole means of employment. Many are driven to seek out further compensation for the meagre earnings they receive at the hands of a noble and supposedly respectable employer. Take the glove makers of Worcester, who in their respectable daylight trade will work an average rate of sixteen hours a day, six days a week, receiving only four shillings in return. Out of that, she must pay one shilling and tuppence for the silk to make her gloves and the remaining two shillings and ten pence is left to pay for lodgings, coal, candles and to *subsist* upon!

It is of little surprise that such circumstances drive out into the owl-light the young women of Worcester! And yet their employers are afforded every comfort and luxury whilst railing against the Great Social Evil they themselves have created. Is it any wonder that the year 1871 saw Manchester record some three thousand women as known prostitutes? Until industry pay meets the needs of its workers, other industries will flourish, driven by necessity.

The Dangers of Prostitution

Nightly, I have sought the comfort of the women who roam the districts of our metropolis, with little to fear of the dangers of the streets. But what of the women themselves? What dangers do they face choosing a life of immorality? Many would have you believe that they are rejected, denied the comfort of family hearth and home because of their tainted nature. And yet, do we not see women of this sort across the city, the country, nay, across the world?

In every corner the sisterhood of the 'unfortunate' thrives and yet is equally reviled by her surrounding fellows. What unfairness do we exact on those whose only fault is to give in to our innate animal passions? None have suffered more than the inhabitants of the East End in this regard. The autumn of 1888 will forever be known as the 'Autumn of Terror' as Jack the Ripper stalked the streets of Whitechapel and left his mark on almost a baker's dozen of the poor women who worked there. In chilling measure, little followed for their protection as a mere four years later saw another rash of murders taken from the ranks of these working women.

Dr. Thomas Neill Cream was charged and hanged for the murder by poison of three women – Matilda Clover, Ellen Donworth and Alice Marsh – and the attempted murder of one more – Louisa Harris – in a violent spree known widely as 'The Lambeth Poisonings'. All had been unfortunates and had been poisoned by strychnine after Dr. Neill had accompanied them home from a music hall. He was only caught because of his attempts to exhort money from reputable men by writing to them claiming to know they had committed the murder. These letters were passed to the police and their detailed knowledge of the crimes revealed them to be the work of none other than the murderer himself. A search soon identified Dr. Neill as the man responsible. The shiftless blaggard attempted to pass the blame on to another student in his lodgings, but his guilt was assured and he was rightly imprisoned for his timely appearance in court. Great excitement greeted his trial, but I do not think any persons present would blame the women of the East End for extracting some small amount of joy at its deadly outcome, a meagre justice to suit the absence of that owed to those who died at Jack the Ripper's hands.

The arguments of the 'Great Social Evil' have gripped every person in our great nation, from Prime Minister to Pauper. Legislation has attempted to control and suppress, or control and legitimise, but I hope, as our century draws to a close, that we have departed from the older arguments built on the belief that prostitution was a necessity to protect virtuous women from men's untameable lusts. The Bishop of Manchester has denied that prostitution is desirable either for services to a standing army or for the development of manhood.

Illustrated Police News, 19 November 1892

Of course, some still argue that there is a social necessity for prostitution if it were held, as some physical philosophers seemed to hold, a need for every lawless passion of our natures to be gratified, but this necessity for prostitution arose from the vicious and unbridled passions which men allowed to grow in their hearts. What we see now are the passions and dedications of men and women across the country in securing the rescue and redemption of those unfortunate women of society.

Reports abound from Manchester of midnight meetings that are held to reclaim fallen women, many of whom say it is the 'drink' that has caused their ruin. Several blame the city's Belle Vue Gardens for specifically aiding them in their downfall and I am sure such reports have given a healthy boost to the numbers of patrons now calling the Gardens their home. Committees across the country have been taking action to set up temporary homes for those women willing to lead a new life, and decent, good people do great work to rescue those in the greatest danger, fighting to place laws and consequence on those who exploit the most innocent members of our society.

But when all is said and done, I remember with fondness my time spent at Madam D'Alma's, sure in the knowledge that for all the societies' good work, there are some women, such as the redoubtable Cora Pearl, who, quite frankly, will not wish to be saved.

Sappho and her Followers

I remember the first time I viewed *Le Sommeil – The Sleepers* – that sensual and seductive work by Gustave Courbet. He had painted it in 1866 for a private collector whom I happened to visit one evening in Paris. As I stared up at the oil-painted canvas the figures upon it seemed filled with life. Two women lay naked on a bed. One dark-haired, her head thrown back in sleep or pleasure I have never been sure, her leg entwined over the body of her female companion, whose blonde curling hair trailed down her chest, tantalizingly, as if about to fall on her companion's naked breast. While I enjoyed the work for my own pleasure, I became increasingly aware that the figures on the bed had little interest in my tastes, as so clearly depicted was their physical love for one another.

This took me somewhat by surprise and I wrote of my curiosity to my friend 'Walter', who answered that he had himself only recently learnt of the existence of physical love between members of the female sex, as there was between males. He wrote to me of his discovery, which had happened while he was visiting a brothel in Paris, having become enamoured of a young lady by the name of Camille, who was educating him in the ways of love:

for the first time with her, I understood that women could, and did, frig themselves; and...placing herself my finger there, I first knew the exact spot where a woman rubs for her solitary pleasure. She told me of women rubbing their clitoris together so as to spend – what the French call tribadism – and two women of her acquaintance did this. The two girls on top of each other I thought a bawdy amusement, and did not believe until after years, that it was practicable, and practiced, with sexual pleasure.

I believe women such as these to be akin to the followers of Sappho, the ancient Greek poet, who was born on the isle of Lesbos, who preferred the company of women and whose life has led to the creation of the word 'Lesbian'.

The Lesbian Mania
Lesbia hath some Cochin China fowls,
Of most superior breeding;
Every one too fat to fly,
So constantly she keeps them feeding.

Lesbia longed to see the show,
Held lately in the street called Baker,
And so importuned me to go,
That I at length was glad to take her.
Curious breeds were there on view –
'Silver-pencill'd' – 'golden-crested'
'Double-comb'd,' I noticed too –
I'd much prefer them double-breasted!

Sodomites: -

It is not just the women who ply a physical trade. The metropolises of the world are rife with houses and clubs that cater to those who indulge in a taste for deviant sexual acts. Most keep their practices out of the public eye, as such interaction is forbidden by law, but occasionally reports appear of congregations of these individuals being discovered by officers of the law. In 1880 the Manchester police raided a fancy ball and arrested 47 persons under the charge of soliciting and inciting each other to commit sodomy and with conspiring to assemble for that singular purpose. Evidently, the police believed acts of the grossest indecency were being committed.

But are there any who think these practices should be accommodated? Some of our greatest literary minds have argued in favour of those who indulge

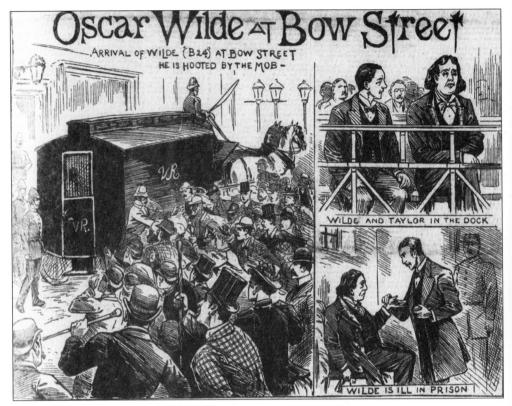

Illustrated Police News, 20 April 1895.

in these very acts. Sir Richard Francis Burton, that most intrepid of travellers, who brought back from the exotic lands of the east *The Karma Sutra,* in 1883 and *The Book of the Thousand Nights and a Night* in 1885, argued that we must not forget that the love between men *'has its noble and sentimental side'*.

And who can forget the moving declaration given by Oscar Wilde during his most unfortunate trial and later imprisonment in 1895 for the revelations of his relationships with a number of younger men? Few would not know it was his love for Lord Alfred Douglas, son of the vile Marquis of Queensbury, which led to Wilde's prosecution. And it was of their relationship that Wilde gave this impassioned defence in court:

A great affection of an elder for a younger man as there was between David and Jonathan, such as Plato made the very basis of his philosophy, and such as you find in the sonnets of Michelangelo and Shakespeare. It is that deep, spiritual affection that is as pure as it is perfect. It dictates and pervades great works of art like those of Shakespeare and Michelangelo… It is in this century misunderstood, so much misunderstood that it may be described as the 'Love that dare not speak its name,' and on account of it I am placed where I am now. It is beautiful; it is fine; it is the noblest form of affection. There is nothing unnatural about it. It is intellectual, and it repeatedly exists between an elder and a younger man, when the elder man has intellect, and the younger man has all the joy, hope and glamour of life before him. That it should be so the world does not understand. The world mocks at it and sometimes puts one in the pillory for it.

Wilde faced a two-year imprisonment with hard labour for his conviction in the strength of *'the love that dare not speak its name'*, and his release after serving the full term occurred in darkness, removing him from the shore of England until his untimely death in Paris a mere three years later. How we punish those whose only crime is to pursue their own natures!

The Cleveland Street Scandal

Some years before the revelations of Oscar Wilde was the discovery and exposure of a brothel at 19 Cleveland Street, Fitzrovia, London, involving a group of Post Office telegraph messenger boys and some of the wealthiest and most influential men in our government. I remember the British press being rocked by the case, known at the time as 'The West End Scandal Case'. The boys were arrested and their subsequent conviction of exceptionally light sentences (well beneath the required two years' hard labour) was met with disbelief. It led to some corners of the press to purport that the leniency shown was due to the involvement of the boys with persons whom the government regarded as its own.

Such accusations were met with denial and libel actions. Take Henry Fitzroy, Earl of Euston, for example. Although he was seen by several witnesses visiting 19 Cleveland Street he launched proceedings against any newspaper who alluded to his involvement. However, the papers refused to be silenced and in 1890 Ernest Parke, of the *North London Press*, appeared in court to answer to a charge of publishing a false and defamatory libel, naming Fitzroy as a frequenter of the house.

A number of witnesses came forward in Parke's defence, all able to place the Earl of Euston at the Cleveland Street brothel on more than one occasion, but none of the witnesses' evidence was more convincing than that of John

Saul. He was a young man, then living in Soho, who had begun to live at 19 Cleveland Street just after Christmas, 1886. His role within the house was to take the gentleman who had entered home after their visit. In May 1887, when in Piccadilly, he had met a gentleman, whom he pointed out to the court as Lord 'Euston', although, Saul claimed, he was well known by another name to those in the locality as the 'Duke'. They had smiled and winked at each other and Lord Euston spoke to him. They drove to 19 Cleveland Street in a hansom and there he and Lord Euston had been guilty of engaging in improper conduct.

This admission caused a great deal of sensation in the courtroom. Saul was then cross-examined by Sir Charles Russell – who, it may interest you to learn, had also acted in *defence* of the boys convicted in the first trial and was now acting as prosecutor against Mr. Parke – and admitted that he was known to have lived a criminally immoral life in Dublin and at various houses in London. The police in Piccadilly had always treated him kindly and let him go up and down unmolested. Saul protested that there were a great many young men in Piccadilly who carried on the same practices as he did.

But when the case against Parke was proved and he was sentenced to 12 months' hard labour, this – and the sentence received by the boys in the first case – gave fuel to the most alarming accusations of a governmental conspiracy. They were taken so seriously that Mr. Henry Labouchère, Liberal MP for Northampton, raised the matter in the House of Commons. It resulted in his exclusion from Parliamentary duties for one week. I do not believe he raised the issue out of any feelings of solidarity or unfairness on behalf of the treatment of the men and boys involved as it was Labouchère who amended the Criminal Law Act of 1885 to prohibit acts of 'gross indecency' between men. He made sure that:

> *Any male persons who, in public or private, commits, or is party to the commission of, or procures or attempts to procure the commission by any male person of, any act of gross indecency with another male person, shall be guilty of a misdemeanour, and, being convicted thereof, shall be liable, at the discretion of the Court, to be imprisoned.*

Before this point, only the crime of sodomy has been prosecutable, between any sex and was far more difficult to prove. Labouchère turned the power of the law specifically on those with a predilection for love of their own sex and branding them the very worst of criminals.

Lord Arthur Cleveland's Advice for Extreme Tastes

Boarding School Boys

It has always surprised me that such strict measures were enacted on the physical interaction of the male sex, given that so many of our fine government men are the former students of those renowned educational houses of the single sex. I too was educated at one of the finest establishments for young boys this country has provided and spent my youth in the company of my fellow sex. It was here, as was common for others in my experience, that I first encountered lewd talk and became aware of the sexual natures of men.

A great friend of my youth recently published a memoriam of the time we spent together during our school days, entitling it *My Secret Life,* and taking it upon himself to disguise his identity behind the pseudonym of 'Walter' – I mentioned him earlier. Some have suggested his true name to be Sir Henry Spencer Ashbee, but I will never be drawn on whether this is, or is not, the truth. The time we spent together saw us initiated into a group of like-minded fellows who had invented a schoolyard game called 'Cocks-all-around', whereby we all found our way into a privy far from the master's eyes and there compared our private parts.

It was here that I first indulged in the terrible act of masturbation, although we referred to it in the schoolboy slang of 'frigging', although we were all terrified of the dangers, being told often by our schoolmasters and fathers that it would lead only to death or insanity. I found it to be a most enjoyable sensation. There were boys who would frig each other, but as I grew older I had little interest in such shared experiences, seeing them merely as the natural adventures of youth. My tastes were drawn far more to the female sex and I intended to procure a physical union with them by any means possible.

Breach of Promise

Although it is not in my nature to be deceitful, the art of love is often a game and draws from the inexperienced lover unwise promises made in the heat of passion. What man has not declared his love, his unquenching desire for the woman he loves; who has not been driven mad by her refusal to satiate both their lusts without the comfort of a wedding ring? It is not always the case that we would choose our lovers from the free and gay women of the world, or wish to part with money to get them.

Sometimes, it is love alone which drives us, not merely lust. In some instances, this can lead to an unwise connection and a promise of marriage made to secure a physical union – for some reason there exist certain noodle-headed females who believe that a promise is as good as a ring and will take to the marriage bed before the legal proceedings have passed. In such circumstances, it is not unusual to find a sudden cooling in her lover's ardour once he has had her and the poor girl will find herself abandoned and ruined to boot.

But this is one small moment when the law will not deny her absolution and any man foolish enough to break an acknowledged promise of marriage will find himself liable to be sued for damages in the public courts. This knowledge I would pass on to any young man who believes that a promise of marriage is a means to an end and something to be offered without consideration. I am fascinated to read of the cases so often brought before the courts on this subject and keep a scrapbook of the ones of most interest, excerpts of which I leave below, to act as deterrent to my reader.

Sheffield Daily Telegraph, 1877: -

> *In the Under-Sheriff's Court at Leicester Castle on Tuesday, Annie Bridget Cartwright, forewoman to a mantle and dressmaker, sued Charles Taylor, pawnbroker, for damages for breach of promise of marriage. The engagement commenced in 1872, and it was understood by both parties that the wedding was not to take place for two years. It was postponed for an additional year because the defendant had just entered into partnership, his father having supplied him with £100 capital, and it was necessary that he should see how it paid first. Defendant was accused of flirting with another girl, and this he denied up to six weeks of the marriage, when he married another young lady. There was virtually no defence. The jury found for the plaintiff, damages £250.*

Nottingham Evening Post, 1882: -

> *A farmer's widow, named Roberts, residing near Aberystwyth, sued a neighbouring farmer, named Hughes, at the Glamorganshire Assizes, yesterday, for breach of promise of marriage. It was alleged by the plaintiff that she had been repeatedly promised marriage by the defendant, and that on the 6th of August last she was seduced by him, and was now enceinte. Damages were laid at £1000. The defendant denied the promise through his legal representative, but was not sworn. The jury found a verdict for the plaintiff – damages, £150.*

Western Times, 1885: -

Lord Arthur Cleveland's Advice for Extreme Tastes

A lady who has been head of an educational institution with a high sounding name, was awarded £200 yesterday as solatium for breach of promise of marriage. She had sued for £5,000. From the love letters produced it appeared that the defendant, if 'a man of means and substance', was not exactly a gentleman of taste. He had promised the lay that when they were 'spliced' they would live 'in slap-up style'. The damages were evidently given for only the loss of 'means and substance'.

Derby Mercury, 1887: -

At the Sheriff Court, York, on Thursday, an action for breach of promise of marriage was brought by Clarissa Miller, spinster, of Burton Salmon, near Milford, against Henry Fletcher, railway clerk, of Knaresborough. After keeping company for about four years the defendant said he had found somebody better, and refused to marry the plaintiff. He only earned 17s. 6d. wages, and was ordered to pay £7. 10s. Damages.

In 1895, there was an extraordinary case brought by a young actress Catherine Kempsall, also known as Mrs. West, against a Liverpool gentleman who did well to keep his name out of the papers. She claimed £10,000 damages for the defendant's breach of promise to her, declaring that he had promised to settle £100,000 on her and convinced her to give up the stage which, being her profession, had provided her income. But it was the reported scenes in the courtroom that were the most extraordinary elements of the case, as:

the plaintiff suddenly attempted to jump over the counsel's bench to get at the defendant. She was seized...but her struggles were so violent that it was necessary for the officers of the court to come to the warder's assistance. The plaintiff screamed and kicked, calling out 'Beast! Beast!' and was carried downstairs screaming and kicking all the way.

Let that be a warning to you, my diligent reader – when it comes to marriage be prepared to put your money where your mouth has pledged you.

Brothels

When our young Queen first took to her throne there were, for a short period of time, revelations in the press against the Dean and Chapter of Westminster. It was revealed that within their parish, 24 houses that were owned by the ecclesiastical body were operating as notorious and renowned brothels. This

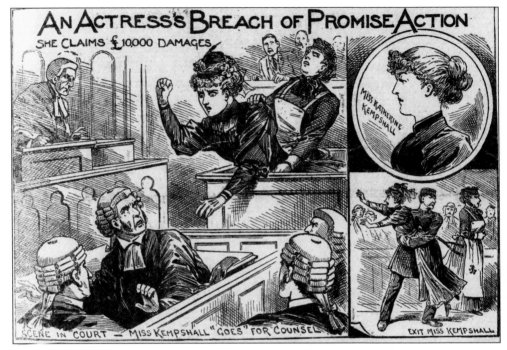

Illustrated Police News, 10 August 1895

admission was met with a strict rebuttal by the Bishop of London who announced that all had been closed and the illicit trade would be suppressed in future. I think such a claim to be both ignorant of the nature of human beings and ignorant of the nature of London. In the reign of Henry VII there were 18 of these famous brothels operating in London and for a time, in order to appease certain parties, the king forbade them. But soon afterwards 12 were allowed to return to their trade and had signs painted on their walls – the Boar's Head, the Cross Keys, the Gun, the Castle, the Crane, the Cardinal's Hat, the Bell, the Swan, etc.

Since that time houses such as these have continued with more or less prosperity and I think it next to an impossibility to suppress them utterly. In the 1850s the parish of St James was only half a mile long and three-quarters of a mile broad, but held within that space were 105 brothels. Turning away from London, to those great sites of industry towards the North, the year of 1862 saw Liverpool record 686 brothels and 2194 prostitutes. And almost a decade later, Manchester stated that it held over 300 bawdy-houses, which catered to all tastes of the trade.

In my youth, the Queen of the immoral trade in London was none other than Mrs. Theresa Berkley, of 28 Charlotte Street, Portland Place. She was a mistress of the art of love, suffering from a great deal of good humour, which she would use to extract from her client his every letch, whim, caprice and desire so as to see them gratified. Her enterprising nature led in 1828 to the construction of a machine to which she lends her name, 'The Berkley Horse', built for gentlemen to be flogged upon. Capable of being opened to a considerable extent, it allows any angle of the body to be reached and is used alike by men and women. This and other such eroticism were offered at Charlotte Street and, I do not doubt, in similar houses of disrepute.

It has been a constant source of discussion in our press and parliaments, reform societies and ecclesiastical gatherings, to decide what should be done about the brothels and industry of prostitution. Some are for repression, some are for legislation. I wonder if we should look to Paris and see the emergence of a legal trade? On my last visit I returned home with a number of tokens from the houses there.

Parisian Brothel Tokens, late 1800s. Artist: Steven Kirk

On the face of some is the visage and name of the lady who you wish to visit, while on the back, her address, and the time and length of your appointment. Some bear the image of a crown, which is a particular favourite of mine as I occasionally visited '*Le Chabanais*', one of the most sumptuously decorated brothels in Paris, just after the panels of galloping centaurs had been painted there by Henri de Toulouse-Lautrec in the 1890s. *Le Chabanais* deserves its glorified reputation as it was rumoured to have served none other than the Prince of Wales, Albert Edward, heir apparent to our beloved Queen.

During his visits of the 1880s and 1890s – shortly after I had myself returned from Europe – the Prince had constructed a special chair, specifically to suit his purpose, that is, for him to enjoy two lovers simultaneously. This '*siège d'amour*' was constructed in a delicate, yet sturdy, design, with ornate green and gold embroidered fabric cushions and beautifully wrought metal foot holders, to give greater purchase for those who occupied it. It was a thing of true beauty and much admired by all who came across it.

But sadly, this is not Paris and our brothels do not run with the support of the law. Do you wonder what the punishment is for those keeping a disorderly house? Surprisingly, for much of our century it has been the prerogative of the

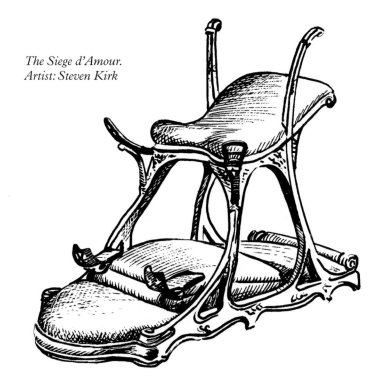

The Siege d'Amour.
Artist: Steven Kirk

public to police them, as prosecutions against persons keeping bawdy-houses were only possible if two inhabitants of any parish or place gave notice *in writing* to any constable (or other peace officer of like nature, where there is no constable) of any person *keeping a bawdy-house,* gaming-house, or any other disorderly house in their locality. Only then, on receipt of the sworn statement of information, would the police be under any duress to act against such establishments, which otherwise – as long as they operated quietly and caused no nuisance to their neighbours – were able to carry out their trade with little interference.

I am not now, nor have I ever been, an advocate for the making of a crusade on the brothels of our nation. It must be understood by all of those in reasonable society that such houses will exist, and have existed, since time immemorial. The law should only punish those who act against the better natures of man; others should be allowed to exist freely, as they have done for many generations before.

The English Vice

It seems a preoccupation of our nation to be disposed to flagellation. And this final word for those to whom the bawdy-house is a commonly sought home, on the fashion which has existed throughout our time, what the French call *les vice anglais* – The English Vice. Flagellation is present in every nursery and school across the land, as a form of childish discipline. And yet, on entering adulthood, there seems to be a desire by some members of our society to experience birching in a very different manner.

The brothels of which I have already spoken, have drawn a ready trade in this fetish. One establishment I visited kept an extensive supply of birch, always in water, so that it remained green and pliant: there were shafts with a dozen whip thongs on each of them; a dozen different sizes of cat-o'-nine tails, some with needle points worked into them; various kinds of thin bending canes; leather straps like coach races; battledores, made of thick sole-leather with inch nails run through the docket; and currycomb tough hides rendered callous by many years' flagellation.

There were also holly brushes; furze brushes; a prickly evergreen called butchers bush; and during the summer, glass and china vases filled with a constant supply of green nettles. For those whose desire it was to birch a woman, rather than to be birched by her, there were a number of ladies in attendance who would take any number of lashes the flogger pleased. Amongst them were Miss Ring, Hannah Jones, One-Eyed Peg and a girl called Ebony Bet.

But it was not only in the brothels and immoral houses that such activities have persisted. In my experience I have personally known of several ladies of high rank who had an extraordinary passion for administering the rod and who took great pleasure in such actions. And I witnessed myself the heated debate carried out between the pages of the *Englishwoman's Domestic Magazine*, whereby the correspondence between 'Pro-Rod' and 'A Lover of Obedience' espoused the emotions and joy they had felt whilst being subjected, and subjecting others, to the punishment of birching.

I am not entirely sure, however, if the esteemed publication in question was not somewhat misused by those writers, who perhaps diverted the discussion of childhood discipline to a more sensual debate. Moreover, that honourable English churchman of the Oxford Movement, Edward Bouverie Pusey, advises his followers to practise self-flagellation 'for about a quarter of an hour a day' to remind oneself that 'our bodies become sacred; they are not ours'. It seems as if all our vices have become virtues, and when such a holy advocate recommends it, should we really have ever called it a vice at all?

In Conclusion

I hope you have enjoyed this weird and wonderful journey through the attitudes and ideas of the Victorian century. Perhaps you have been shocked or surprised by just how modern many Victorian attitudes appear to be. With any luck, this book should have gone some way towards challenging the beliefs we all have about the nineteenth century, from ideas on sex, and women, to pleasure and marriage.

We often only think of Victorian sexuality as a battleground between a dominant patriarchy and a supposedly submissive female counterpart. But as women like Annie Besant, Cora Pearl and Ada Lovelace have shown us, that is not the case. Although difficult to fully express when writing as a Victorian, Ada's correspondence with Charles Babbage – the father of modern computer programming – is highly significant. So the Victorians were highly anti-women, but in reality this century is full of incredibly strong female figures either excelling in their chosen fields – literary or scientific – or campaigning to improve conditions for womankind.

So where do our misconceptions of the Victorian attitudes to sex come from? I'm not sure; ever since the nineteenth century ended there seems to have been an overwhelming desire to paint the Victorians as repressed, or sexually deviant, but I just don't think that is the case. In *The Technology of Orgasm*, Rachel P. Maines argues that the late Victorian medical fraternity would often submit hysterical women to 'pelvic massage' to cause what she describes as a 'hysterical paroxysm' or orgasm. She believes that the popular vibration devices of the time, such as the '*VeeDee Vibrator*', took the place of this manual labour on the part of the doctors who were unaware that the reaction they were provoking in their patients was in any way linked to their sexuality. This has become a popular theory for the press and media but one for which supporting evidence is a little thin on the ground.

As we have seen, the Victorians were fully aware of the female orgasm and the effects of masturbation and so it is highly unlikely that a doctor would carry out this practice without the knowledge that it was a sexual act. I have also not yet found a single reference to a specific 'pelvic massage' in any of the books or pamphlets I have read on the treatment of hysteria in Britain, or directions for how it would be carried out, let alone the later use of vibration in this area.

However, while I disagree with Maines's theory of a widespread medical practice, I do not doubt that some enterprising Victorians would have privately used the device in this way; I mean after all, look at '*Vigor's Horse-Action Saddle*', or the *Femme de Voyage*! Objects like this are almost impossible to find now, and as sex has always been regarded by the majority of society as a personal and private affair, it is almost impossible to gauge how many people were openly exploring their sexuality with their partner. The price of the *Femme de Voyage* gives us a clue about its popularity. Although the guinea coin was abandoned in 1816 and replaced by the pound, it was still a term that remained in use throughout the nineteenth century, most often in conjunction with goods for the high end of the market. A guinea is equal to 21 shillings, and in modern money this places the *Femme de Voyage* as costing £300, or upwards of £12,000 by the end of the century. This would have placed it out of reach of most people living in the Victorian period and so, as with the *Siege d'Amour*, possibly only available – if it does, in fact, exist – to royalty.

But that doesn't mean that sexual exploration was only the property of those with money. Annie Besant and Charles Bradlaugh specifically targeted the working classes with their *Fruits of Philosophy* contraception manual, and this is something where we *can* see a widespread impact – there are newspaper reports of hundreds of people clamouring for a copy and a circulation of a reported 125,000 shows us that the average everyday Victorian was just as excited and interested in sex as our own modern society.

For me, the Victorian tenets of True Love, Respect, and Mutual Physical Pleasure are ones we can still embrace today. They are a set of Victorian Values that we *should* identify with, and while the study of Phrenology, or the diagnosis of Hysteria has thankfully been left to the mists of time, there's still an awful lot we can thank the Victorians for. After all, we wouldn't have the Kama Sutra, rubber condoms, or the age of consent without them.

For the Historian

This is by no means a complete list of all the sources available, but merely those that have directly influenced the text. The list is presented on a chapter by chapter basis.

With the exception of the *Taranaki Herald*, which is taken from the National Library of New Zealand Te Puna M tauranga o Aotearoa, all newspapers are sourced from the British Newspaper Archive (*www.britishnewspaperarchive .co.uk*) and used with their kind permission.

Introduction

Newspapers
'The Contagious Diseases Acts', *London Daily News*, 28 December 1869
'Special Correspondence: Letter from Mrs Butler', *The Shield*, 25 April 1870
'The Maiden Tribute to Modern Babylon', *Pall Mall Gazette*, July 1885
'The Eliza Armstrong Case', *Manchester Evening News*, 8 September 1885
'The "New Journalism"', *Sunderland Daily Echo and Shipping Gazette*, 19 August 1887

Books and Pamphlets
A Guide to Marriage, 1865, Manchester: Albert Sidebottom
The Lover's Guide to Courtship and Marriage, 1883, London: R. March & Co.
Booth, Charles. *Life and Labour of the People in London*, three editions, published 1889–1903, London: Macmillan and Co.
Mayhew, Henry. *London Labour and the London Poor*, 1851, London
Tissot, Samuel Auguste David. *A Treatise on the Diseases produced by Onanism*, 1832, New York: Collins & Hannay. (Edition produced after Tissot's death in 1797, first published 1758.)
N.B. – *On Onanism:* There is an early work from 1716 which discussed why masturbation is a negative practice, but as Tissot's had a resounding influence throughout the Victorian century, I would argue it is the more important.

Volume 1: Dr. Dimmick's Guide to the Anatomy

Newspapers

'Celibacy in West Devon', *Western Times*, 1 January 1842

'Dr. Kahn's Anatomical Museum', *Morning Chronicle*, 27 July 1853

'Indictment of the Proprietor of an Anatomical Museum', *Bradford Observer*, 19 January 1854

'Dr. Kahn's New Museum and Gallery of Science', *The Era*, 6 December 1857

'Dr Kahn and "The Lancet"', *The Era*, 28 February 1858

'The Nottingham Lace Factories', *Nottinghamshire Guardian*, 28 July 1859

'Sir David Brewster on Physiognomy', *Dublin Evening Mail*, 6 November 1862

'Guy's Hospital. The Medical Session Commences in October', *Northampton Mercury*, 29 August 1868

'A Masculine Young Lady', *Paisley Herald and Renfrewshire Advertiser*, 3 December 1870

'Raid on An Anatomical Museum', *Dundee Courier*, 4 March 1873

'A Manchester Anatomical Museum', *Manchester Evening News*, 28 May 1874

'The Protection of Young Girls', *Derby Daily Telegraph*, 25 July 1882

'Correspondence', *Northern Echo*, 6 May 1889

'Physiognomy★', *Morning Post*, 20 January 1891

'Notes on News', *Yorkshire Evening Post*, 26 March 1891

'Young Men Who Are Got Up', *Huddersfield Chronicle*, 4 April 1893

'The Masculine Girl', *Blackburn Standard*, 14 October 1893

Books and Pamphlets

Excessive Venery, Masturbation and Continence, 1883, London: Birmingham & Co.

A Guide to Marriage, 1865, Manchester: Albert Sidebottom

Brown, H. '*Advice to Single Women Regarding Their Health with Hints concerning Marriage*', 1899, London: James Bowden

Kellogg, J. H. *Plain Facts For Old and Young*, 1881, Iowa: Segner & Condit

Simms, Dr. J. *Nature's Revelations of Character; or, Physiognomy Illustrated. A description of the Mental, Moral and Volitive dispositions of mankind, as manifested in the human form and countenance*, 1879, New York: D.M. Bennett

Stanton, Mary Olmstead. *Physiognomy. A practical and scientific treatise*, 1881, San Francisco: San Francisco News Company

Von Krafft-Ebing, R. Baron. *Psychopathia Sexualis, with especial reference to antipathic sexual instinct…The only authorised English translation of the tenth German edition*, 1899, Translated by Francis J. Rebman, London: Rebman

Volume 2: Mrs. Dollymop's Advice for the Single Lady

Newspapers

'Middlesex Sessions, April 24th', *London Standard*, 25 April 1850

'General News', *Nottinghamshire Guardian*, 20 January 1859

'The Social Evil in Paris', *Dundee Advertiser*, 21 April 1864

Huddersfield Chronicle, 21 July 1866 (Chambers' Journal)

'Woman', *Sheffield Daily Telegraph*, 22 January 1877

'Woman's Love', *Evening Telegraph*, 12 October 1878

'Points of Difference between Men and Women', *The Sunderland Daily Echo and Shipping Gazette*, 13 March 1884

'The Life of Cora Pearl', *Edinburgh Evening News*, 30 March 1886

'The End of Cora Pearl', *Edinburgh Evening News*, 12 July 1886

'Mrs Besant's Beliefs', *Portsmouth Evening News*, 14 November 1889

Manchester Courier and Lancashire General Advertiser, 7 July 1890

'Fan Flirtation', 'Parasol Flirtation', *Taranaki Herald*, 1891

'Florence Nightingale', *Manchester Courier and Lancashire General Advertiser*, 13 July 1894

'The New Woman', *Tamworth Herald*, 14 July 1894

'Josephine Butler's Reminiscence', *Hastings and St Leonard's Observer*, 17 October 1896

Books and Pamphlets

Etiquette of Marriage, 1857

A Guide to Marriage, 1865, Manchester: Albert Sidebottom

The Lover's Guide to Courtship and Marriage, 1883, London: R. March & Co.

Brown, H. *'Advice to Single Women Regarding Their Health with Hints concerning Marriage'*, 1899, London: James Bowden

Delvau, A. *Les Plaisirs de Paris: guide pratique et illustre*, 1867, Paris: A. Faure

Knowlton, C. *Fruits of Philosophy: An essay on the population question ... Second new edition, with notes (signed: George Drysdale, the preface signed Charles Bradlaugh, Annie Besant)*, 1877, London: Freethought Publishing Co.

Website

Quotation taken from *Queen Victoria's Journals Online*, Volume 13, 10 February 1840, p. 349 (RAVIC/MAIN/QVJ (W) (Princess Beatrice's copies), accessed 27 August 2013 (*www.queenvictoriasjournals.org/home.do*)

Volume 3: The Reverend J.J. James's Advice for the Single Man

Newspapers

'Eye Flirtation', 'Glove Flirtation', 'Hat Flirtation', *Taranaki Herald*, 1891
'The King Of Strong Men', *Dundee Courier*, 27 January 1898
'Eugen Sandow's Greatest Invention', *Edinburgh Evening News*, 7 April 1900

Books and Pamphlets

A Guide to Marriage, 1865, Manchester: Albert Sidebottom
The Lover's Guide to Courtship and Marriage, 1883, London: R. March & Co.
Humphry, Charlotte, E. *Manners For Men*, 1897, London: James Bowden
Knowlton, C. *Fruits of Philosophy: An essay on the population question ... Second new edition, with notes (signed: George Drysdale, the preface signed Charles Bradlaugh, Annie Besant)*, 1877, London: Freethought Publishing Co.

Artefacts

Artefacts from the Museum of London

Volume 4: Lady Petronella Von-Hathsburg's Guide to Marital Relations

Books and Pamphlets

Etiquette of Marriage, 1857, kept in the Museum of London
A Guide to Begetting Handsome Children, 1860, kept in the Museum of London
A Guide to Marriage, 1865, Manchester: Albert Sidebottom
Teller, J., *Dr Teller's Pocket Companion, or Marriage Guide: being a popular treatise on the anatomy and physiology of the genital organs, in both sexes, with their uses and abuses; together with a complete history of secret diseases, their causes symptoms and treatment, in plain language devoid of all technicalities*, 1865, New York
Knowlton, C., *Fruits of Philosophy: An essay on the population question ... Second new edition, with notes (signed: George Drysdale, the preface signed Charles Bradlaugh, Annie Besant)*, 1877, London: Freethought Publishing Co.
The Lover's Guide to Courtship and Marriage, 1883, London: R. March & Co.

Volume 5: Mr. Mandrake's Practical Aids

Newspapers

'Answers to Correspondents', *The Girls Own Paper*, 12 July 1884
'Hysteria', *Hearth and Home*, 4 May 1893
'Proved By Cures', *Hull Daily Mail*, 5 March 1897
'Massage', *The Girls Own Paper*, 16 June 1900

For the Historian

Books and Pamphlets

Madam B★★. *La Femme Endormie*, 1899, Australia: J. Renold

Beard, G.M. *Sexual Neurasthenia [Nervous Exhaustion]. Its Hygiene, Symptoms, and Treatment, with a chapter on Diet for the Nervous.* 1884, New York: E.B. Treat & Co.

Bloch, I., *'The Sexual Life of our time in its relation to Modern Civilization'* 1909, London, Rebman Limited (Originally written in Germany 1906 and published as *'Das Sexuallenben unserer Zeit in seinen Beziehungen zur modernen Kultur'*.)

Champneys, F.H. *On Painful Menstruation. The Harveian Lectures*, 1890 (with Tables), 1891, London: H. K Lewis

Dick, H., *Gleet: Its Pathology and Treatment*, 1858, London: H. Bailliere

Finger, Dr. E. *Gonorrhoea: Being the Translation of Blenorhoea of the Sexual Organs and Its Complications*, 1894, New York: W. Wood

Grose, F. Lexicon Balatronicum. *A dictionary of Buckish slang, University wit, and Pick Pocket eloquence… Altered and enlarged… by a member of the Whip Club*, 1811, London

Granville, J. M. *Nerve-vibration and excitation as agents in the treatment of Functional disorder and Organic Disease*, 1883, London: Churchill

Howe, J.W. *Excessive Venery, Masturbation and Continence*, 1883, London: Birmingham & Co.

Merck's Manual of the material medica, together with a summary of therapeutic indications and a classifications of medicaments: a ready-reference pocket book for the physician and surgeon, 1899, New York: Merck & Co.

Pharmacopoeia of the London Lock Hospital, 1887, London: Adlard & Son

The Slang of Venery, 1916, privately printed

Teller, J., *Dr Teller's Pocket Companion, or Marriage Guide: being a popular treatise on the anatomy and physiology of the genital organs, in both sexes, with their uses and abuses; together with a complete history of secret diseases, their causes symptoms and treatment, in plain language devoid of all technicalities*, 1865, New York

United States Practical Receipt Book, or Complete book of reference, for the manufacturer, tradesman, agriculturalist or housekeeper; containing many thousand valuable recipes, in all the useful and domestic arts, 1844, USA: Lindsay & Blakiston

Artefacts

Artefacts from the Museum of London and the Science Museum Archive at Blythe House.

Volume 6: Lord Arthur Cleveland's Advice for Extreme Tastes

Newspapers

'The Dean and Chapter of Westminster and Their Brothels', *Morning Chronicle*, 29 June 1844

'Compulsory Prostitution', *Reynolds's Newspaper*, 15 February 1852
'Poetry', *Yorkshire Gazette*, 18 February 1854
'Prostitution in London', *Paisley Herald and Renfrewshire Advertiser*, 23 January 1858
'The Immoral Traffic in Belgian Girls', *Morning Chronicle*, 28 November 1861
'The Suppression of Brothels', *Liverpool Mercury*, 9 January 1862
'The Traffic in Immorality', *Lloyd's Weekly Newspaper*, 11 September 1870
'Prostitution in Manchester', *Manchester Evening News*, 25 October 1871
'Breach of Promise', *Sheffield Daily Telegraph*, 21 July 1877
'Police Raid On A Fancy Ball', *Staffordshire Sentinel*, 30 September 1880
'Inveigling English Girls Abroad', *Manchester Evening News*, 17 December 1880
'The Immoral Traffic in Girls', *Worcester Chronicle*, 23 April 1881
'Breach of Promise', *Nottingham Evening Post*, 21 February 1882
'Breach of Promise', *Western Times*, 20 June 1885
'Summary', *Derby Mercury*, 28 December 1887
'The London Scandals', *York Herald*, 16 January 1890
'Lambeth Poisonings', *Lloyd's Weekly Newspaper*, 23 October 1892
'The Execution of Dr Neill Cream', *Illustrated Police News*, 19 November 1892
'Breach of Promise', *Leeds Times*, 3 August 1895
'Alleged Immoral Traffic in Chinese Girls', *Illustrated Police News*, 17 June 1899

Books and Pamphlets
'Consideration', Criminal Law Amendment Bill, *Hansard*, 6 August 1885
Englishwoman's Domestic Magazine, 1875
The Slang of Venery, 1916, privately printed
Pisanus Fraxi (Ashbee, Henry Spencer), *Index Librorum Prohibitorum: being notes bio-biblio-icono-graphical and critical...on curious and uncommon books*, 1877, London: privately printed.
'Walter', *My Secret Life*, 1888. Amsterdam Believed to the diaries of Henry Spencer Ashbee (1834–1900) recounting his sexual life from boyhood onwards. They were banned due to their explicit nature and it was not until 1995 that the work was published in its entirety, without censorship or prosecution, in Britain.

Website
Transcript of Oscar Wilde's 1895 trial, published online University of Missouri-Kansas City Law School.

Artefacts
Articles held in the Museum of London

Index

Index